THE ART *of* BELIEVING

A JOURNEY TO A PEACEFUL LIFE

Dr. Sunita Raaj

BlueRose ONE.com
Stories Matter
NewDelhi • London

BLUEROSE PUBLISHERS
India | U.K.

BlueRose ONE
Stories Matter
NewDelhi • London

For permissions requests or inquiries regarding this publication, please contact:

BLUEROSE PUBLISHERS
www.BlueRoseONE.com
info@bluerosepublishers.com
+91 8882 898 898
+4407342408967

ISBN: 978-93-5989-365-5

Cover design: Tahira
Typesetting: Tanya Raj Upadhyay

First Edition: April 2024

Table of Contents

Part I: Meticulous Aspects

Part A: The Art of Believing

I. Introduction

The Art of Believing: A Journey to a Peaceful Life is an inspiring and empowering book that offers practical advice and guidance on how to transform our thoughts and beliefs, into a more powerful, peaceful, and fulfilling life. It encourages readers to tap into their inner potential to create the life they have always wanted. Through simple, yet effective techniques, this book will help readers gain clarity, develop positive habits, and learn to trust their intuition to make better decisions.

A. Meaning of "The Art of Believing"

The art of believing involves embracing **faith, trust, and optimism.** It is the ability to have confidence in **a higher self, oneself, others, and the world around us.** Belief provides a framework for **thinking positively** and **taking actions** that align with our **goals and aspirations.**

Meaning of belief: Acceptance that something **exists or is true**, especially one without proof, is often referred to as faith. Faith is the belief in something beyond what can be seen or proven, relying instead on trust and conviction. It can be a powerful force that guides individuals through **difficult times, inspires hope,** and **provides comfort.**

Whether faith in **a higher power, in oneself, or the goodness of others,** it serves as a beacon of light in the darkness, offering solace and strength. Embracing faith can bring **a sense of peace and purpose,** helping individuals navigate the **uncertainties of life with courage and resilience.**

"Trust, faith, or confidence in (someone or something)."

The term "**believe**" typically refers to the act of accepting or holding something to be **true or correct** without definitive **proof or evidence.** It involves having **faith, trust, or confidence** in something or someone, usually based on **personal convictions**, **experiences, intuition, or religious or philosophical principles.** Belief often implies a firm conviction or acceptance of a particular **idea, concept, or viewpoint,** even in the absence of **concrete proof.**

"Let's take a closer look at the meaning of the word - Belief: Be + Lief"

Be means to exist, to live, to occupy a place in the world. It is the essence of our very being, the core of our existence. To be is to experience all that life has to offer, to feel emotions, to form connections with others, and to grow and evolve as individuals.

It is a state of constant flux, as we navigate through the highs and lows of our journey. Being is not just about existing **physically,** but also about thriving **mentally, emotionally, and spiritually.** It is about embracing all that we are and all that we can become.

Lief means to live with love and kindness in our hearts. It means to treat others with compassion and empathy, to spread positivity wherever we go.

Lief is about embracing the beauty of life and all the wonderful moments it brings. It encourages us to be grateful for the small joys and to cherish our relationships with others. **In essence,** to embody lief is to live a life filled with warmth, connection, and joy.

"Enjoy The Peaceful Journey of Life by Learning

-The Art of Believing."

Scripts on Belief:

"If you can?" said Jesus. ***"Everything is possible for one who believes."*****-Mark 9:23**

"But when you ask, you must believe and not doubt, because the one who doubts is like a wave of the sea, blown and tossed by the wind." **-James 1:6**

"Truly I tell you, if anyone says to this mountain, 'Go, throw yourself into the sea,' and does not doubt in their heart but believes that what they say will happen, it will be done for them". -**Mark 11:23**

"Therefore I tell you, whatever you ask for in prayer, believe that you have received it, and it will be yours." **-Mark 11:24**

"But those who hope in the ***Lord*** *will renew their strength. They will soar on wings like eagles; they will run and not grow weary, they will walk and not be faint."***-Isaiah 40:31**

"If you believe, you will receive whatever you ask for in prayer." **-Matthew 21:22**

"The future belongs to those who believe in the beauty of their dreams."-**Eleanor Roosevelt**

"The way we think shapes our reality, so choose positive thoughts and watch your life transform."-**BK Sr. Shivani**

"Whatever the mind of man can conceive and believe, it can achieve."-**Napoleon Hill**

*"Faith consists in believing when it is beyond the power of reason to believe."***-Voltaire**

B. Overview of the concept "The Art of Believing"

Belief is an essential part of the human experience. It allows us to make sense of the world and our place in it. But it can also be a **powerful tool** to help us create a better life for ourselves and those around us. That's why I'm going to share with you this book **"The Art of Believing"—a journey to a peaceful life.**

To believe in something, we must first have faith in it. Having faith in something means trusting that it is possible and that it will work out. We must also accept that it is our responsibility to make it **happen** and **take action** toward making it happen.

Believing begins with a **mindset of openness and receptiveness**. It requires us to let go of **doubt and negative thoughts,** and instead, hold onto the idea that **anything is possible.** Believing in ourselves means **recognizing our potential and having the courage to pursue our dreams, good health, and a good life, even in the face of challenges and setbacks.**

Believing in others is essential for **fostering meaningful relationships** and **building strong communities.** It is about seeing the inherent goodness and potential in those around us and offering support and encouragement to help them thrive. By believing in others, we inspire them to **believe in themselves, creating a positive ripple effect.**

Believing in the world involves maintaining a hopeful outlook and having faith in the greater good. It means **recognizing** that, **despite the chaos and adversity** we may face, there is **beauty, compassion,** and **progress** happening all around us. Believing in the world also motivates us to contribute to its betterment, whether through **acts of kindness, environmental stewardship, or social change**.

The art of believing requires **practice and cultivation**. It involves **nurturing a positive mindset through self-reflection, gratitude, and mindfulness, reprogramming the subconscious mind.** Surrounding ourselves with **like-minded individuals** who share our beliefs can also be empowering and reinforcing.

Ultimately, **The Art of Believing is a transformative force** that can lead to **personal fulfillment, empathy, and a greater sense of purpose.** It enables us to **overcome obstacles, connect with others, and make a positive impact in the world.**

C. "The Art of Believing" Why is this book essential for the reader?

The book **"The Art of Believing"** is essential for any reader because it offers **powerful insights and techniques to harness the power of belief.** Belief plays a crucial role in shaping **our thoughts, emotions, and ultimately our actions.** Through this book, readers can learn how to **cultivate positive and empowering beliefs that can transform their lives.**

One key reason why this book is essential is that it helps readers **understand the impact of belief on achieving success and happiness to lead a peaceful life.** Exploring various examples and case studies demonstrates how individuals who believed in themselves and their goals were able to overcome obstacles and achieve remarkable results. This book **provides a roadmap** for readers to tap into their belief systems and unleash their true potential.

Moreover, **"The Art of Believing"** delves into the **psychology behind belief** and **how it influences our perception** of reality. By **understanding the power of belief** and its role in shaping our thoughts, readers can **challenge and change old limiting beliefs** that may be holding them back. This book **provides practical exercises and strategies** to **reframe negative beliefs**, **cultivate self-confidence, and develop a positive mindset.**

Furthermore, **"The Art of Believing"** is essential for readers **seeking personal growth** and **self-improvement.** It offers valuable lessons on **developing a growth mindset and embracing a belief system** that fosters **continual learning and growth.** The book emphasizes the importance of **self-**

belief and **provides techniques to silence self-doubt** and **cultivate resilience**

In summary, **"The Art of Believing"** is an essential book for any reader because it provides valuable **insights and techniques to harness the power of belief.**

Whether one is **seeking success, happiness, personal growth, improving the relationship with one another, having a healthy lifestyle, or simply a more positive mindset,** this book offers **practical strategies to cultivate empowering beliefs and transform one's life.**

II. What is "The Art of Believing"?

Belief is an inherent part of human life, as we grow and mature, we come to believe in various aspects of life. It has been **an essential aspect of human consciousness** for centuries, and its roots can be traced back to the **earliest human civilizations.**

Belief is often shaped by **our environment, culture, and experiences.** Whether it's a religious belief or a belief in ourselves, it can have a significant impact on our lives. Believing in something **gives us purpose and direction, pushing us to strive towards our goals and aspirations.**

However, belief can also be **a double-edged sword.** It can lead to close-mindedness and division among communities with conflicting beliefs. It's **essential to acknowledge and respect others' beliefs**, even if they **differ from our own.**

Ultimately, belief is a powerful tool that can shape **our thoughts, actions,** and **perspectives on life.** It's up to us to **use it wisely and with kindness towards ourselves and others.**

A. History of "The Art Of Believing."

The concept of **"The Art of Believing"** has been a fundamental part of human existence since the beginning of time. It has played a pivotal role in shaping different cultures, religions, and societies throughout history. Belief is a powerful force that has been **used to explain unexplainable conceptions, give hope, provide comfort, and inspire greatness.**

The history of belief is a long and complex one, spanning across different cultures, religions, and societies. Belief has played a vital role in shaping our world, inspiring us to achieve great things, and providing us with comfort and hope during difficult times. It continues to be an integral part of human existence, and its impact will undoubtedly continue to shape our world for generations to come.

The Evolution of Belief Throughout History.

In ancient times, belief systems were primarily rooted in **animism and polytheism.** Animism is the belief that all natural objects, such as trees, rivers, and animals, possess a spiritual essence or soul. Polytheism, on the other hand, involved **the worship of multiple gods and goddesses,** each associated with different aspects of life.

As human societies became more complex, belief systems began to evolve. One significant turning point in the development of belief was the emergence of **monotheism.**

Monotheism is the belief in **a single supreme deity,** who is **all-powerful, all-knowing, and eternal.** This concept gained prominence in various civilizations, such as ancient Egypt with the worship of Aten and later in Judaism, which influenced Christianity and Islam.

In more recent times, a decline in religious beliefs has been observed in some parts of the world due to advancements in science, secularization, and the rise of atheism and agnosticism. However, belief systems continue to be deeply ingrained in **the human experience, shaping personal identities, moral values, and worldviews.**

Overall, the history and origins of belief systems are complex and intertwined with various cultural, political, and societal factors. **They reflect humanity's search for meaning, purpose, and understanding of the world around us.**

B. Explanations of the Core Principles of "The Art of Believing"?

The core principles of **"The Art of Believing"** revolve around cultivating a mindset that promotes self-belief and the ability to manifest one's desires. These principles encourage individuals to tap into their subconscious mind and harness the power of their beliefs to create positive outcomes in their lives.

Here are some of the core principles of the art of believing.

1. The power of belief can serve as a driving force for creativity.

The art of believing proposes that beliefs are **not just a reflection of reality,** but they **actively shape and create reality.** Individuals can manifest their desires and shape their lives by cultivating positive and empowering beliefs.

When we believe in ourselves and our abilities, we are more likely to take risks and think out of the box. This can **lead to new and innovative ideas.** Belief can also give us **the motivation and perseverance** to see our **creative sides.** Even when we are faced with challenges or setbacks.

Additionally, belief in the impact and value of our creations can inspire us to share them with others and make a positive impact on the world. So, whether it's belief in **ourselves, our ideas, or a higher power, harnessing the power of belief can be a powerful tool for unlocking our creative potential.**

Let's spotlight Rohni's story: how the power of belief can ignite creativity and open doors to countless possibilities.

The town girl Rohni came to the city to practice her design skills. She was filled with self-belief and determination, knowing that she had the talent and passion to succeed. Despite the initial struggles and doubts she faced in adapting to the fast-paced city life, Rohni held onto her belief in her creativity.

Through her unwavering faith in herself, she pushed past her comfort zone and explored new avenues for inspiration. She found beauty in the chaos of the city, drawing inspiration from the vibrant colors and diverse cultures that surrounded her.

With each design she created, Rohni poured her belief into her work, infusing it with her unique perspective and creative flair. Her belief in the power of her creativity not only propelled her forward but also inspired others to believe in their creative abilities.

As Rohni's designs gained recognition and praise in the competitive city scene, she remained humble and attributed her success to her unwavering belief in the **transformative power of creativity.**

Through her journey, she exemplified how the power of belief can fuel creativity and pave the way for endless possibilities.

2. Belief has the power to reprogram the subconscious mind.

The subconscious mind is a powerful force that influences **thoughts, emotions, and behaviors. The art of believing**

emphasizes the need to reprogram the subconscious mind by replacing old limiting beliefs, negative self-talk, and self-doubt with positive and empowering beliefs and thoughts.

For instance: When we have **negative self-talk** and **limiting beliefs**, it can hold us back in many aspects of life. It can cause us to doubt ourselves and our abilities, making it difficult to achieve our goals.

By reprogramming our subconscious mind, we can change the ways we think and feel about ourselves, others, and our surroundings. This involves identifying our negative thought patterns and replacing them with positive ones. Through repetition and consistency, we can create new empowering beliefs that will help us reach our full potential and create our own desired beautiful destiny.

The art of believing is not just about positive thinking, it's about taking action to change our beliefs and transform our lives.

Arpana's Story: From Dreaming to Achieving

Arpana Rakesh aspired to launch a vegetarian restaurant. She believed in her cooking and serving skills, despite the lack of facility she had. She started small, cooking for friends and family, and receiving positive feedback that fueled her belief in her dream.

Despite facing challenges and setbacks, her unwavering belief in herself and her vision helped her secure a small space where she could start her vegetarian restaurant. With every step she took, she found herself in a big dilemma. The challenges seemed insurmountable at times, and self-doubt whispered in her ear.

But Arpana chose to silence those doubts with determination and perseverance. She sought advice from successful restaurateurs, honed her culinary skills through courses and workshops, and meticulously planned every aspect of her restaurant.

Through hard work and dedication, Arpana's vegetarian restaurant finally opened its doors to the public. The aroma of her delicious dishes filled the air, attracting customers from near and far. Her dream had transformed into a reality, a testament to the power of believing in oneself and taking decisive action to make those beliefs come true. After seven years of dedication, she received multiple rewards from the local government.

Arpana's story serves as an inspiration to all who dare to dream and are willing to put in the effort to turn those dreams into tangible achievements. It reminds us that the art of believing goes beyond mere positive thoughts; it requires courage, persistence, and a willingness to step out of our comfort zones to create the life we envision for ourselves.

Through dedication, hard work, and a positive mindset, Arpana's belief not only reprogrammed her subconscious mind but also transformed her dream into a successful reality.

In the subsequent chapters, you will learn various techniques for reprogramming the subconscious mind. These techniques include visualization, meditation, Self-hypnosis, positive self-talk, etc.

Each of these methods can be used to tap into the power of the subconscious mind, which will provide you with a better understanding to create positive everlasting changes in your life.

Belief indeed holds transformative power over the subconscious mind, shaping our thoughts and actions in profound ways. By consciously practicing the art of believing, we pave the way for personal growth and success.

3. Belief Can Influence Visualization and Imagination

Visualization and imagination are key techniques in **"The Art Of Believing".** By vividly imagining desired outcomes and mentally rehearsing them, individuals can enhance their belief in achieving them and attract them into their lives.

When we visualize something, we create a mental image in our mind. This can be a powerful tool in achieving our goals because our subconscious mind cannot differentiate between a real experience and a vividly imagined one. By continually visualizing our desired outcome, we can send a signal to the universe that we truly believe in our ability to achieve it. **This positive energy can then attract the necessary resources, opportunities, and people into our lives to make our vision a reality.**

For instance, using visualization in sports. Athletes often use mental imagery to help them prepare for competitions. They imagine themselves performing at their best, winning their event, and receiving their medal. This helps them stay focused and motivated and enhances their belief in their ability to achieve their goals.

The techniques of visualization and imagination are incredibly powerful tools that can also be used in **many aspects of life such as health, wealth, good relationships, personal development, career, financial stabilities, etc.**

For instance, if someone wants to improve their confidence, they can imagine themselves in various situations where they would typically feel nervous or unsure.

By mentally rehearsing these scenarios and visualizing themselves as confident and capable, they can enhance their belief in their abilities and ultimately become more confident in real-life situations.

Ankita's Story of Visualization: The Journey of Recovery and Healing.

Ankita had a chronic illness, breast cancer and she was visualizing her betterment. Ankita's dedication to visualizing her healing process day by day not only illustrates her strong belief in her recovery but also showcases the power of the mind in influencing outcomes.

Through her persistent visualization of a healthier self, she was not only boosting her morale but also sending out positive vibrations to the universe. This act of harnessing the power of belief through visualization can have a profound impact on her journey towards wellness.

As Ankita continued to imagine herself in a state of well-being, she was paving the way for her body to respond positively to this optimistic mindset. The universe, in turn, aligned in support of her vision and brought forth healing opportunities, treatments, and individuals who aided her in her path to recovery.

Ankita's story serves as a testament to the remarkable connection between belief, visualization, and the manifestation of our deepest desires.

The book comprehensively covers the techniques of visualization and imagination in a subsequent chapter. As you progress through the book, your understanding of these techniques will undoubtedly improve.

4. Belief forms the foundation of our desires and aspirations.

Belief indeed plays a significant role in shaping our desires and aspirations. It can provide the motivation and conviction needed to pursue our goals, guiding us toward what we believe is achievable and meaningful.

To materialize and manifest our desires and aspirations, it's crucial to synchronize our thoughts, beliefs, and actions with our desired outcomes. This involves consciously choosing the right thoughts and beliefs that align with our objectives and consistently taking actions that bring us closer to our goals.

It is also important to stay open to opportunities and be willing to take risks that may lead to the desired outcome. This may involve stepping out of our comfort zone and trying new things, as well as being persistent and determined in the face of obstacles.

Mr. Rick Desired to Provide Top-Quality Education for His Daughter on a Modest Income.

Mr. Rick aimed to provide his daughter with the best education, even though it was expensive compared to his modest income. He worked tirelessly, taking on extra shifts and saving every penny possible to ensure his daughter had the educational opportunities she deserved.

He believed wholeheartedly in the power of education and he was determined to make it a reality for his daughter. Despite his challenges, his unwavering belief in the importance of learning kept him motivated and focused on his goal.

His dedication and perseverance paid off in the end, as his daughter excelled academically and went on to pursue her dreams, inspired by her father's unwavering belief in her potential.

In the end, it was not just about providing her with an education but instilling in her the belief that anything is possible with exertion and determination.

Ultimately, **manifesting desires** requires a combination of a **positive mindset and profound action. By aligning right and elevated thoughts, beliefs, and actions with what is desired, we can create a powerful force that attracts those desires into reality.**

5. The Crucial Role of Belief in Fostering Self-Awareness and Self-Reflection

"The Art of Believing" encourages individuals to develop **self-awareness** and engage in **self-reflection** to identify and confront any negative beliefs, doubts, or fears that may hold them back. By understanding and addressing these old limiting beliefs, individuals can strengthen their self-belief and overcome obstacles.

Through **self-awareness**, individuals can become more conscious about their thoughts, emotions, and behaviors, and how these impact their beliefs about themselves and the world around them. **Self-reflection** allows individuals to examine their **beliefs and thought patterns** and **determine** if they align with the right values and goals.

By embracing this mindset and working on self-awareness and self-reflection, individuals can cultivate a strong sense of self-belief and achieve their goals and aspirations.

For instance, One's beliefs play a crucial role in fostering self-awareness and self-reflection, especially when it comes to health. Individuals can significantly impact their overall well-being by cultivating a strong belief in the body's ability to heal and thrive.

Embracing positive beliefs about health and wellness can empower individuals to make healthier choices, adopt positive habits, and seek out the support they need to lead a balanced and fulfilling life.

Believing in the body's innate ability to heal and regenerate can be a powerful motivator for taking care of oneself. This belief can inspire individuals to prioritize self-care practices, such as exercise, proper nutrition, rest, and stress management.

Furthermore, having a positive outlook on health can help individuals navigate challenges and setbacks with resilience and determination.

In essence, fostering a belief in the body's capacity for health and vitality can serve as a foundation for overall well-being. **By nurturing this belief through self-awareness and self-reflection, individuals can embark on a journey towards a healthier and happier life.**

Exploring more about **Self-Awareness and Self-Reflection** in the subsequent chapters provides comprehensive coverage of the topic of Belief in Self-Awareness and Self-Reflection. As you delve further into the text, your grasp of these concepts.

6. Beliefs provide the foundational value for gratitude and a positive mindset.

Gratitude and maintaining a **positive mindset** are essential in the art of believing. Expressing gratitude for what we already have and focusing on the positive aspects of life helps foster a belief in abundance and attracts more positive experiences.

When we concentrate on our **deficiencies or lack of resources,** we create a belief in scarcity and attract more negativity to our lives. However, when we shift our focus to what we're grateful for and what's going well in our lives, we cultivate a belief in abundance and attract more positivity in our lives.

Illustration: Imagine a boy who constantly complains and finds faults in everything.

Despite having a loving family and all the comforts he could ask for, the boy's constant complaints and focus on what he lacked created a negative mindset that overshadowed his blessings.

Instead of cherishing what he had, he always yearned for more, perpetuating a belief in scarcity. If only he could shift his perspective and appreciate the abundance surrounding him, his mindset would transform, and he would attract even more positivity into his life.

It's a powerful reminder that gratitude and positivity are integral to shaping our beliefs and ultimately our experiences.

In the subsequent chapters, we will delve deeper into the concept of Gratitude and explore ways to nurture and sustain a positive mindset to manifest the desired life.

By cultivating a grateful heart and mind, we can cultivate a positive outlook that attracts abundance and joy. Through simple yet powerful practices, we will learn how to shift our focus towards the blessings in our lives, no matter how small, and create a ripple effect of positivity that enhances our well-being. Get ready to embark on a journey of self-discovery and transformation as we unlock the secrets of gratitude together.

7. The strength of belief lies in sustaining persistence and resilience.

"The Art of Believing" acknowledges that the process of manifesting desires may not always be **smooth or immediate**. It emphasizes the importance of **persistence and resilience** in the face of setbacks or challenges, as maintaining a strong belief in one's abilities and desired outcomes is crucial for success.

Maintaining a strong belief can be likened to tending a garden. **Just as a gardener must nurture their plants with consistent care and attention, individuals must cultivate their beliefs through persistence and resilience.**

Each setback or challenge can be seen as an opportunity for growth and learning, rather than a roadblock to success. By staying committed to their beliefs and remaining resilient in the face of adversity, individuals can navigate through obstacles and ultimately achieve their desired outcomes.

The art of believing is not just about having faith, but also about actively working towards one's goals with unwavering determination and a positive mindset.

A Story of Persistence and Resilience: A Journey from Struggling to Gaining Recognition, Let's Embark on How Ms. Aditi gained professional recognition.

Ms. Aditi, a French teacher, faced challenges in gaining professional recognition at first. Her perseverance and resilience shone through, leading her to become recognized as the top French teacher in a prestigious school.

Ms. Aditi's dedication to her French teaching passion was unwavering, despite the initial hurdles she encountered. She spent countless hours refining her teaching techniques and engaging her students in a way that was both educational and inspiring.

Her passion for the French language and culture was contagious, and soon her students were not only excelling in their language skills but also developing a deep appreciation for the beauty of the French language.

As word spread about Ms. Aditi's innovative teaching methods and her ability to connect with her students on a personal level, she started to gain the recognition she deserved. Colleagues and school administrators alike began to take notice of the remarkable transformation happening in her classroom.

With each passing day, Ms. Aditi's confidence grew, and her impact on her students became even more profound. She became a mentor to other teachers, sharing her knowledge and insights to help them improve their teaching practices.

Ms. Aditi's journey from struggling to gain recognition to being celebrated as the top French teacher in the school was a testament to her persistence and resilience. Her story inspired not only her students but also everyone around her to harness the art of believing and never give up on their dreams, no matter how difficult the path may seem.

In Topic Conclusion

Overall, **“The Art Of Believing”** encourages individuals to become **conscious creators of their reality by harnessing the power of belief and aligning their thoughts, emotions, and actions with their desired outcomes.** By adopting these core principles, individuals can unlock their potential, enhance their self-belief, and manifest their desired life.

C. What are the pillars of “The Art of Believing”?

The pillars of “The Art of Believing" are as follows:

The concept of **"The Art of Believing"** doesn't have universally established pillars like some other philosophical or belief systems do. Yet, to delve into this concept, one can contemplate the following potential pillars as a starting point.

1. Faith:

Belief often begins with faith in something, whether it's **a religious deity (supreme power, God), a personal goal, or an ideology. Faith is the foundation upon which belief is built.**

It is the invisible force that propels us forward, the unwavering trust in the unseen and the unknown. Faith gives us the courage to take that first step into the darkness, knowing that there is light waiting to guide us.

In times of uncertainty and doubt, faith acts as our steadfast companion, whispering words of hope and resilience. It is the beacon that shines brightest in our darkest hours, reminding us that we are never truly alone.

So let us nurture our faith, for it is the seed from which our dreams blossom and our spirits soar. Embrace it, cherish it, and let it lead you on a journey of discovery, growth, and endless possibilities. With faith as our compass, we can navigate the vast expanse of life's mysteries with unwavering determination and unwavering belief.

2. Conviction:

Believing requires a strong sense of conviction. It's not just about passive acceptance but having a deep, unwavering belief in something. Conviction empowers us to stand firm in our beliefs, even in the face of challenges and doubts.

It gives us the strength to pursue our dreams and goals with unwavering determination. When we hold onto our convictions, we exude a sense of purpose and confidence that inspires others to believe in themselves too. Let our conviction be the guiding force that propels us towards success and fulfillment.

3. Imagination:

Imagination can play a significant role in believing. It allows you to envision the possibilities and outcomes of your beliefs. Imagination is a powerful tool that can fuel your beliefs and aspirations. By tapping into your creative mind, you can explore different scenarios and visualize the potential results of your beliefs.

This process not only helps us stay motivated and focused but also enables us to see beyond the present moment and aim for a brighter future. Embrace your imagination, for it can turn your beliefs into reality.

4. Commitment:

Belief often requires commitment and dedication. It's not enough to merely believe; you must be willing to act on your beliefs and invest time and effort in them to have a desired positive outcome. Commitment is like the fuel that drives your beliefs towards fruition.

It is the steadfast resolve to stay true to your convictions, even when faced with doubt or uncertainty. By investing your time and effort into what you believe in, you are laying the foundation for a brighter and more fulfilling future.

Remember, commitment is not just a word; it is a mindset, a way of life. It is the conscious choice to stay committed to your beliefs, no matter how tough the journey may get. So, embrace commitment wholeheartedly, for it is the bridge that connects your beliefs to your reality, turning dreams into accomplishments.

5. Resilience:

Believing in something can indeed be a challenging journey, as doubt, skepticism, and adversity may try to cloud your vision. However, it is during these moments that resilience becomes your greatest ally. Resilience allows you to stay strong and unwavering in your beliefs, even when faced with obstacles and challenges.

It is the inner strength that helps you persevere, overcome doubts, and continue to hold onto what you believe in, no matter what comes your way. Resilience is like a muscle that grows stronger with every trial you overcome. It is the ability to bounce back from setbacks, doubt, skepticism, or adversity.

Remember, it is often through adversity that our beliefs are truly tested and strengthened. So, stay resilient, have faith in yourself and your higher self, and trust in the power of your beliefs to guide you through any storm.

6. Open-mindedness

While belief is important, being open-minded to new ideas and perspectives can help refine and strengthen your beliefs over time. Embracing open-mindedness allows us to expand our horizons, challenge our assumptions, and grow both intellectually and emotionally.

By being receptive to new ideas and perspectives, we can engage in meaningful conversations, enrich our understanding of the world, and cultivate empathy toward others. Open-mindedness encourages us to question our beliefs, and seek out diverse viewpoints, and evolve our perspectives based on new information and experiences.

It is a valuable trait that fosters creativity, innovation, and personal growth, ultimately leading to a more enriched and fulfilling life.

7. Self-reflection:

Regular self-reflection allows you to assess the validity and impact of your beliefs. It's a crucial aspect of the art of believing. Taking the time for regular self-reflection is like looking in the mirror of your mind.

It allows you to explore the depths of your beliefs, understand their roots, and evaluate their influence on your thoughts and actions. Engaging in this practice can lead to personal growth and a deeper sense of self-awareness, helping you navigate through life with more clarity and intention. Remember, the art of believing starts with knowing yourself.

Other Important Pillars of "The Art of Believing" are as follows:

Talent: Talent is a natural ability or skill that a person possesses. It is something that comes naturally to them, without much effort or training. Talents can be in various areas such as music, art, sports, academics, or any other field. Talents are often recognized and appreciated by others and can be nurtured and developed to achieve excellence.

Passion: Passion is an intense and compelling enthusiasm or desire for something. It is a strong emotion and drive that motivates an individual to pursue and dedicate themselves to a particular interest, goal, or activity.

Passion often involves a deep enthusiasm and enjoyment of the subject or activity, and individuals who are passionate about something often devote a significant amount of time and energy to it. Passion can manifest in various aspects of life, including hobbies, relationships, career choices, or personal pursuits.

Hard work: Hard Work refers to the consistent and dedicated effort put into completing a task, project, or goal. It involves a high level of focus, perseverance, determination, and willingness to go the extra mile to achieve success. Hard work often requires sacrificing personal time, overcoming challenges, and putting in long hours to accomplish desired results.

Love and Compassion: Love and Compassion is a deep feeling of empathy and sympathy for others, often accompanied by a desire to alleviate their suffering or help them in some way. It involves understanding and connecting with the emotions and struggles of others, and it plays a crucial role in fostering kindness and cooperation among individuals and in building a more compassionate society.

Self-healing power: Self-healing power is a remarkable ability that resides within each one of us. It is the innate capacity of our bodies to repair, regenerate, and restore balance to maintain overall health and well-being. By believing in the wisdom of your body and allowing it to guide you on a path towards greater Vitality.

The concept of "Self-Healing" will be further explored in the subsequent chapters. There you can understand more about the remarkable ability of our bodies to repair and rejuvenate themselves.

By gaining a better understanding of these concepts, you will be equipped with valuable insights on how to optimize your body's natural ability to heal and thrive. Stay tuned for an enlightening journey into the world of self-healing and well-being.

In Topic Conclusion:

Remember that **"The Art of Believing"** is a highly subjective and personal concept, and these pillars can vary significantly depending on individual beliefs and philosophies. However, some common themes often serve as pillars within the belief concept. Each person's unique combination of these pillars contributes to their art of believing.

It is important to remember that there is no right or wrong way to cultivate this art, as it is a deeply individual journey that evolves. Embracing your own beliefs and staying true to yourself are key elements in **Mastering The Art Of Believing.**

D. The psychology behind " The Beliefs".

The psychology behind belief can be **complex and influenced** by a variety of factors. Some key aspects are given here, you can refer to the psychology behind the beliefs.

1. Cognitive processes:

Belief formation often involves **cognitive processes such as perception, attention, memory, and reasoning.** Our interpretation of information and experiences can shape our beliefs, as well as cognitive biases and heuristics that influence how we process and evaluate information.

For instance, When it comes to **perception,** our beliefs can be influenced by how we perceive the world around us. Our **attention** to certain details or information can also impact the **formation** of our beliefs, as well as our **memory** of past experiences that contribute to our belief systems.

Furthermore, **reasoning plays** a crucial role in belief formation. The way we analyze and make sense of information can either strengthen or challenge our existing beliefs. It is important to be mindful of cognitive biases and heuristics that may lead us to draw inaccurate conclusions or hold onto beliefs that are not supported by evidence.

By understanding the **cognitive processes** involved in belief formation, we can become more aware of how our beliefs are shaped and be open to critically evaluating and refining them based on new information and experiences.

A Story of a young man who experienced a traumatic incident, and how cognitive intervention shaped his behavior.

A young man had a traumatic incident at the age of 18 during a school trip involving water sports. While enjoying the activities, he had a near-drowning experience in the sea but he was fortunately rescued by his teammates.

Now his **cognition** is deeply impacted by that event, leading to a fear of water that influences his beliefs and behaviors. Whenever he encounters situations involving water, his perception is clouded by **memories** of that incident, causing his **attention** to be hyper-focused on the potential dangers rather than the enjoyable aspects. His memory of the traumatic event is vivid, replaying the fear and panic he felt during the near-drowning experience.

As a result, his **reasoning** about water-related activities is skewed, as his cognitive biases amplify the perceived risks and downplay the likelihood of a positive outcome. Over time, these cognitive processes reinforce his belief that water is inherently dangerous, making it challenging for him to overcome his fear and experience water activities without anxiety.

Understanding the role of cognitive processes in shaping beliefs can help individuals become more aware of how their past experiences influence their current beliefs and behaviors, empowering them to challenge and reframe their perspectives for personal growth and well-being.

2. Social and Cultural Influences:

Beliefs are often shaped by **social and cultural factors.** We are influenced by the beliefs of those around us - such as parents, teachers, peers, and society at large. Cultural values and norms can also shape our beliefs, as they provide a framework for understanding the world and guide our interpretations.

For instance, in some cultures, the concept of fate or destiny plays a significant role in shaping beliefs about personal agency and control over one's life. In contrast, other cultures may emphasize individualism and the importance of personal choice and responsibility.

Moreover, cultural values and norms also play a crucial role in shaping our beliefs. Our culture provides us with a set of values, traditions, and customs that influence how we perceive the world around us. These cultural influences act as a guide, helping us interpret our experiences and make sense of the complexities of life.

Ultimately, our beliefs are complex and multifaceted, reflecting a dynamic interplay between individual experiences, social interactions, and cultural contexts. By recognizing the various influences that shape our beliefs, we can cultivate a deeper understanding of ourselves and others, fostering empathy and open-mindedness in our interactions.

Illustration: If a woman is married into a diverse family, how might society and culture influence her?

When a woman marries into a diverse family, society, and culture can play a significant role in shaping her experiences and interactions. In such a scenario, she may have the opportunity to learn about and appreciate different customs, traditions, and beliefs from various backgrounds. This exposure can lead to a greater understanding and acceptance of diversity, fostering open-mindedness and empathy.

Society may also place certain expectations or stereotypes on her based on the cultural backgrounds of her in-laws. She needs to navigate these external perceptions while staying true to her own identity. By embracing her unique cultural heritage and actively engaging with the traditions of her new family, she can contribute to the rich *tapestry of diversity within her household and community.

Ultimately, the influence of society and culture on a woman married into a diverse family can be a source of growth, connection, and mutual respect. It is through that she embraces and celebrates these differences so that she can cultivate a more inclusive and harmonious environment for herself and those around her.

*Tapestry: It is a collection of memories, experiences, and emotions that shape our identity and define who we are.

3. Emotional factors:

Emotions play a role in belief formation and can cause us to be more open to certain beliefs or seek out evidence that supports our existing beliefs. **Emotions are powerful influencers in how we perceive and interpret information.**

When we experience strong emotions, our brains can become more receptive to certain ideas or opinions, leading us to be more inclined to believe in them. This phenomenon can sometimes lead us to actively seek out information that aligns with our emotional state or preconceived beliefs, reinforcing our existing convictions.

It's important to be aware of the impact of emotions on our beliefs, as understanding this connection can help us approach new information with a more open and critical mind.

By recognizing the role emotions play in belief formation, we can strive to maintain a **balance between our feelings and rational thinking, fostering a more well-rounded and informed perspective.**

Illustration: Our emotions have a significant impact on how we form our beliefs and perceive the world around us.

For instance, Fear can lead us to prioritize safety and security, often influencing the beliefs we hold in those areas. Conversely, the desire for a deeper sense of purpose or meaning can guide our beliefs towards spirituality, the afterlife, and our place in the universe.

It's fascinating how our emotional experiences can color the lens through which we view the world, influencing the paths we choose to explore and the convictions we hold dear.

By recognizing the interplay between our emotions and beliefs, we can gain a deeper understanding of ourselves and others, fostering empathy and connection in the process.

A Story of Emotion: Melody Kumar's Journey from Emotional Loss to Liberation

The story of Melody Kumar who lost it all - his marriage, job, and family life. Now, he seeks to begin anew and get back on track. As Melody Kumar stood amidst the ruins of his former life, a sense of despair threatened to consume him. With his marriage shattered, his job lost, and his family life in disarray, he found himself at a crossroads. However, deep within him, a flicker of hope ignited—a determination to rise from the ashes and start afresh.

With each step forward, Melody Kumar embarked on a journey of **self-discovery and renewal.** He delved into his innermost thoughts and emotions, confronting the pain and turmoil that had led him to this point. Through introspection and reflection, he began to unravel the tangled web of his past choices and actions.

As he navigated the tumultuous waters of change, Melody Kumar discovered a newfound resilience within himself. With each challenge he faced, he found the strength to persevere and the courage to confront his inner demons. Slowly but steadily, he started to rebuild his life, brick by brick, laying the foundation for a brighter future.

Through his trials and tribulations, Melody Kumar learned the importance of **resilience, forgiveness, and self-compassion.** He realized that setbacks are not the end but merely stepping stones on the path to **growth and transformation**. With a renewed sense of purpose and a steadfast resolve, he set out to reclaim his lost dreams and redefine his destiny.

And so, Melody Kumar's story became a testament to **the power of redemption and the resilience of the human spirit.** In his journey from loss to liberation, he discovered that it is never too late to rewrite the narrative of his life and create a future filled with **hope, healing, and endless possibilities.**

4. Need for certainty and control:

Beliefs provide a sense of certainty and control over the world, helping us make sense of complex or uncertain situations. They can provide a sense of stability and predictability, which can be comforting in the face of **ambiguity or fear.**

In a world filled with **unpredictability and constant change,** our beliefs act as a guiding light, offering us a sense of stability and control. They serve as a solid foundation upon which we can build our understanding of the world around us. When faced with complexity or uncertainty, our beliefs offer us a sense of direction, allowing us to navigate through challenges with confidence and clarity.

By holding onto our beliefs, we create a framework that helps us interpret our experiences and make sense of the world. This framework not only provides us with a sense of certainty but also empowers us to take control of our lives and make informed decisions. In times of doubt or fear, our beliefs can serve as a source of strength, offering us solace and reassurance.

Ultimately, our beliefs play a crucial role in shaping our perceptions and guiding our actions. They serve as a compass, guiding us through the intricate maze of life and helping us find our way even in the darkest of times.

Embracing our beliefs allows us to embrace the unknown with courage and resilience, knowing that we have **the power to create our sense of certainty and control in an ever-changing world.**

A story of certainty and control: A newly married couple migrating to a different country to begin a fresh chapter in their lives.

A newly married couple migrating to a different country to begin a fresh chapter in their lives. They may rely on their belief in the strength of their relationship to provide them with a sense of certainty and control amidst the uncertainties of a new environment.

This belief can serve as a foundation, guiding them through challenges and unknown territories, offering them reassurance and a shared sense of purpose. In this way, their belief in their love and commitment to each other can act as a beacon of stability, illuminating their path as they navigate the complexities of their new life together.

In navigating the uncharted waters of a new life, beliefs play a significant role in providing a sense of direction and purpose. The couple's unwavering faith in each other acts as a guiding light, illuminating their path and offering them solace in times of uncertainty.

Together, their shared belief in the strength of their bond acts as a powerful force, giving them the courage to face challenges head-on and the resilience to overcome obstacles that may come their way.

As they embark on this new journey hand in hand, their belief in their love becomes not just a source of comfort but a source of strength, propelling them forward toward a future filled with promise and possibility.

They set the road maps for others to follow, inspiring hope and courage in those around them. Despite the uncertainties and challenges that come with starting anew in a foreign land, their unwavering bond serves as a pillar of support, grounding them in times of doubt and fear.

With each obstacle they overcome together, their connection deepens, solidifying their commitment to each other and their shared dreams. The unfamiliarity of their surroundings only serves to strengthen their resolve, as they navigate the unfamiliar with a sense of unity and determination.

Through their journey, they learn that true certainty and control do not come from having all the answers or knowing what the future holds, but from trusting in themselves and in each other to face whatever may come their way with bravery and resilience. As they continue down this path hand in hand, their story of certainty and control evolves into a tale of love, resilience, and unwavering faith in the power of togetherness.

5. Motivational factors:

Our beliefs can be influenced by our motivations and goals. For instance, we may hold beliefs that align with our self-concept or identity, as these beliefs help to maintain a sense of consistency and coherence. Beliefs can also be influenced by our desire to protect our self-esteem or maintain a positive view of ourselves and our abilities.

Another key motivational factor that can shape our beliefs is the need for **belonging and connection.** Humans are social beings, and often our beliefs are influenced by the desire to fit in with a particular group or community. This need for social acceptance can lead us to adopt beliefs that are prevalent within our social circles, even if they may not align with our values or experiences.

Furthermore, other motivational factors in pursuit of personal growth and development can also play a significant role in shaping our beliefs. When we are **motivated to learn, improve, and evolve as individuals,** our beliefs may shift to **accommodate new information and experiences.** This growth mindset can lead us to question previously held beliefs and adopt new perspectives that better serve our ongoing development.

In essence, our motivations and goals serve as powerful drivers that shape our beliefs, influencing how we perceive ourselves, interact with others, and navigate the world around us.

By understanding the motivational factors behind our beliefs, we can gain insight into the complex interplay between our internal desires and external influences, ultimately leading to a deeper understanding of our belief systems.

A story of self-motivation: A boy, Satvick, was determined to overcome his fear of heights.

A boy who was determined to overcome his fear of heights. Despite feeling anxious and unsure, he believed in his ability to conquer his fear. His self-concept as a brave and resilient individual fueled his determination.

With each step closer to the edge of the cliff, he reminded himself of his identity as a fearless adventurer. The belief in his strength and courage provided him with the consistency and coherence he needed to push forward. As he reached the summit and gazed at the breathtaking view below, his self-esteem soared. He had proven to himself that he was capable of facing his fears head-on, strengthening his positive view of himself and his abilities.

As he stood there, the wind gently tousling his hair, Satvick felt a sense of accomplishment wash over him. The fear that once held him back now seemed like a distant memory. He had not only conquered the physical height but also the mental barrier that had been weighing him down.

With a newfound confidence, he made a silent promise to himself - to never let fear dictate his actions again. As he descended from the cliff, a smile played on his lips, knowing that he was capable of achieving anything he set his mind to. The story of Satvick became an inspiration to others, a reminder that with determination, self-motivation, and self-belief, one can overcome even the most daunting challenges.

Spotlight another story of Motivation: Phillips, Whose hidden talent was Acknowledged by His Uncle Raja

Phillips, a newlywed, was facing tough times with financial struggles, unemployment, and the pressure of supporting his family. Amidst this, his uncle Raja was invited by him for dinner to spend quality time with the family. Uncle Raja was impressed by the delicious meal prepared by Phillips, Uncle Raja had an encouraging conversation, suggesting Phillips start a restaurant.

Initially, he was hesitant due to self-doubt and financial concerns, but Phillips gradually embarked on the journey towards his empowerment. Eventually, he successfully opened his restaurant.

Phillips' path was filled with challenges, but he heeded Uncle Raja's words of inspiration, turning them into action. His story stands as a beacon of hope, showcasing how simple words can transform destinies.

Phillips poured his heart and soul into his restaurant, infusing every dish with passion and dedication. As word of his flavorful creations spread, patrons flocked to experience his culinary magic.

With each satisfied customer, Phillips' confidence soared, his initial doubts a distant memory. The thriving restaurant became a testament to his resilience and determination, symbolizing his unwavering belief in himself.

Uncle Raja's wisdom continued to guide Phillips, reminding him that strength lies not just in overcoming obstacles, but in using each challenge as a stepping stone towards greatness. Phillips' journey was not just about opening a restaurant; it was a tale of transformation, of a man who dared to dream and turned his dreams into reality.

And so, under the warm glow of the restaurant's lights, Phillips stood tall, a living testament to the power of belief and hard work. His story served as an inspiration to all who knew him, a reminder that with courage and perseverance, any dream is within reach.

Remember, motivation has the power to change lives. Offer words of encouragement and kindness, as they can make a significant difference in someone's life.

6. Confirmation bias:

People tend to seek information that confirms their existing beliefs while disregarding or downplaying contradictory evidence. This is known as confirmation bias and can contribute to the maintenance and reinforcement of beliefs.

Confirmation bias is a common cognitive bias that affects decision-making and judgment. It can lead individuals to seek out information that aligns with their preconceptions, ultimately reinforcing their beliefs, even if they might not be accurate or supported by evidence.

Recognizing and understanding confirmation bias is crucial in fostering critical thinking skills and promoting open-mindedness. By being aware of this bias, individuals can consciously consider alternative perspectives and evaluate information more objectively.

This practice can help in making more informed and well-rounded decisions, ultimately leading to personal growth and a deeper understanding of the world around us.

For instance, an individual who deeply trusts in self-healing might actively look for articles, books, and stories that endorse self-healing, while disregarding scientific research or medical guidance that contradicts this belief. This selective exposure to information can create an echo chamber where the individual's beliefs are continually echoed and reinforced, further solidifying their conviction in the concept of self-healing.

This echo chamber of selective exposure can lead to a reinforcing cycle where the individual becomes more entrenched in their beliefs, making it challenging to consider alternative perspectives or new information.

While having faith in self-healing can be empowering and beneficial in some cases, it is important to maintain an open mind and critically evaluate information from various sources.

By seeking a balance between personal beliefs and scientific knowledge, individuals can make informed decisions that align with their values while also considering evidence-based practices for their overall well-being.

Conversely, an individual who believes in hospital treatment rather than in self-healing.

Confirmation bias can be a powerful force in shaping our perspectives and influencing our actions. When individuals are predisposed to favor information that supports their current beliefs, they may inadvertently overlook alternative viewpoints or evidence that challenges their assumptions. This tendency can create an echo chamber of ideas, where individuals only hear what they want to hear, reinforcing their existing beliefs without critically evaluating them.

In the example provided, the individual's belief in hospital treatment over self-healing illustrates how confirmation bias can impact decision-making. Despite the potential benefits of exploring alternative healing methods or considering new information, the individual may continue to prioritize information that aligns with their existing belief intervention of hospital treatment. This tunnel vision can limit their ability to make well-informed choices and inhibit their openness to new ideas.

Recognizing the presence of confirmation bias is the first step toward mitigating its influence. By actively seeking out diverse perspectives, remaining open to conflicting evidence, and engaging in critical self-reflection, individuals can challenge their own biases and cultivate a more balanced and nuanced understanding of the world around them.

Embracing intellectual humility and a willingness to reevaluate one's beliefs can ultimately lead to more informed decision-making and a richer, more expansive worldview.

This tendency to selectively process information based on preconceived notions can lead to a distorted understanding of reality and hinder open-mindedness. It is important to be aware of confirmation bias and actively seek out diverse perspectives and evidence to make well-informed decisions from balanced opinions and avoid being trapped in a cycle of narrow-minded thinking.

In Topic Conclusion:

It is important to note that the psychology behind the belief is complex and varies from person to person. These factors can interact and influence each other in different ways, leading to shaping a broad spectrum of beliefs and belief systems.

Understanding the intricate psychology behind belief requires a nuanced approach that takes into account individual differences and diverse experiences. People's beliefs are often shaped by a combination of personal upbringing, cultural influences, education, and life experiences.

These factors can intertwine and evolve over time, creating a rich tapestry of beliefs that contribute to the diversity of perspectives in the world. By recognizing the complexity and variability of belief systems, we can cultivate empathy and open-mindedness towards others, fostering a more inclusive and understanding society.

E. How does an individual evolve around their beliefs and how do they create a belief system?

An individual's evolution of beliefs and the creation of a belief system are complex processes influenced by personal experiences, culture, upbringing, and more.

Exploring the belief system: What is a Belief System?

A belief system can be defined as a set of principles, ideas, values, and attitudes that form the foundation of an individual's understanding of reality. It is a framework that shapes our perception of the world and influences our thoughts, behaviors, and emotions. Our belief systems are formed through a combination of personal experiences, cultural influences, and social conditioning.

Here's how individuals typically evolve around their beliefs and how they create a belief system.

1. Early Influences:

Beliefs often start forming in childhood through the influence of family, caregivers, and cultural surroundings. These early influences shape the foundation of an individual's belief system. We often mention that children mirror their parents. Their way of speaking and comprehending the world is influenced by them. Children learn by observing and imitating the actions and attitudes of those closest to them.

Positive role models who demonstrate kindness, empathy, and respect can help instill these qualities in children. Conversely, exposure to negative behaviors such as abuse, neglect, or dishonesty can have lasting effects on a child's psyche.

Adults need to create a safe and nurturing environment for children to thrive. By fostering an atmosphere of love, respect, and open communication, we can help children develop into individuals who personify compassion, empathy, and kindness toward others.

Through positive reinforcement and guidance, children can learn to navigate the complexities of life with compassion and integrity.

Ultimately, by instilling strong moral principles and teaching the importance of empathy and understanding, we can empower children to become responsible, ethical, and empathetic members of society.

On the contrary, as individuals grow and mature, they may encounter new perspectives and experiences that challenge or reinforce these early beliefs. It is important to recognize the impact of these foundational beliefs on our thoughts, actions, and interactions with others.

By fostering self-awareness and open-mindedness, individuals can consciously evaluate and adapt their beliefs to align with their values and principles, leading to personal growth and positive change.

Remember, it is never too late to reflect on and reshape your beliefs to create a more fulfilling and harmonious life.

2. Personal Experiences:

As individuals grow and gain life experiences, their beliefs can evolve. Positive or negative experiences can challenge or reinforce existing beliefs, prompting a revaluation of their worldview.

For instance, someone who has always believed that people are inherently good may be faced with instances of cruelty or deceit that shake this belief. On the contrary, someone who has held a cynical view of human nature may encounter acts of kindness and compassion that inspire a shift in perspective.

This reevaluation is a natural part of personal growth and self-discovery. It allows individuals to expand their perspectives and develop a deeper understanding of themselves and the world around them.

By remaining open-minded and receptive to new ideas, individuals can continue to evolve and adapt their beliefs in a way that aligns with their values and aspirations. Embracing this ongoing process of self-reflection and growth can lead to greater empathy, compassion, and wisdom, ultimately enriching their lives and relationships.

Alex's bike accident led to a significant change in his perspective.

The young boy Alex, had always believed that he was invincible on his bike, zipping through the neighborhood streets with reckless abandon. That all changed one sunny afternoon when he hit a patch of gravel on a sharp turn, sending him flying over the handlebars and crashing onto the pavement.

As he lay there, dazed and bruised, Alex's belief in his invincibility shattered along his bike. The pain he felt at that moment was not just physical but also emotional, as he realized the fragility of life and how quickly things can change.

Through his recovery, Alex's perspective on biking - and life in general - underwent a profound shift. He began to appreciate the importance of caution and safety, understanding that vulnerability is not a weakness but a reality of being human.

This harrowing experience became a turning point in his life, teaching him valuable lessons about resilience, humility, and the power of personal growth through adversity.

3. Education and Learning:

Formal education, exposure to diverse perspectives, and continuous learning can expand an individual's horizons and lead to the evolution of their beliefs. It encourages critical thinking and the exploration of new ideas.

For instance, individuals who pursue higher education often have the opportunity to engage with a variety of subjects and viewpoints that challenge their existing beliefs. This exposure can help them develop a more well-rounded understanding of the world and foster a willingness to consider alternative perspectives.

In addition, continuous learning throughout one's life allows for personal growth and the refinement of beliefs. By staying curious and open-minded, individuals can adapt to new information and experiences, leading to the evolution of their perspectives over time. This process of growth and development is essential for intellectual and emotional maturity.

By embracing formal education, seeking out diverse perspectives, and committing to lifelong learning, individuals can cultivate a mindset that is receptive to change and growth. This willingness to evolve and expand one's beliefs not only enriches the individual's own life but also contributes to a more inclusive and progressive society.

Envision a story of two boys from the same city, where one is well-educated and the other is not.

The well-educated boy, armed with knowledge and critical thinking skills, embarks on a journey of self-discovery and growth. His education opens doors to a world of opportunities, allowing him to explore different paths and perspectives. With each new piece of information, his understanding of the world deepens, shaping his beliefs and values.

On the contrary, the boy without formal education may find himself limited in his choices and views. Without exposure to diverse perspectives and the tools to critically analyze information, his world remains confined to what he already knows. The lack of education may hinder his ability to adapt to changes and innovate in the face of challenges.

Education is not just about acquiring facts and figures; it's all about developing a mindset that leads to opening the door for learning and growth. It empowers individuals to question, to seek answers, and to continuously evolve. **In a rapidly changing world, education serves as a beacon of light, guiding individuals toward a future filled with possibilities.**

4. Peer Groups and Social Circles:

The people we associate with, such as friends, colleagues, and social groups, can influence our beliefs. Interactions with different individuals may expose us to new viewpoints and challenge our existing beliefs.

For instance, engaging with diverse perspectives can broaden our understanding of the world and help us grow as individuals. By surrounding ourselves with people who have varying opinions and experiences, we can learn to appreciate different viewpoints and develop empathy towards others.

Moreover, our interactions with those around us can also shape our values and attitudes. Through meaningful conversations and debates, we can refine our own beliefs and gain new insights that may have a positive impact on our personal growth and development.

It is important to remain open-minded and willing to listen to different perspectives, even if they differ from our own. By doing so, we can create a more inclusive and understanding community where everyone's voice is heard and respected.

Ultimately, the people we surround ourselves with play a crucial role in shaping our beliefs and influencing our personal growth. By fostering relationships with individuals who challenge us to think critically and expand our horizons, we can continue to evolve and learn from the diverse world around us.

A story of two best friends - The beauty of diversity and the richness of human experiences.

In a bustling city where people of all backgrounds and cultures coexist harmoniously, lived two best friends, Maya and Layla. Maya, with her warm smile and infectious laughter, came from a family rooted in traditional Indian customs, while Layla, with her adventurous spirit and kind heart, had grown up in a household that celebrated Nigerian traditions.

Despite their different upbringings, Maya and Layla shared an unbreakable bond that transcended cultural differences. They spent their days exploring the vibrant city streets, trying new foods, and immersing themselves in each other's customs and traditions. Through their friendship, they discovered the beauty of diversity and the richness of human experiences.

As they navigated life's ups and downs together, Maya and Layla learned valuable lessons about **empathy, acceptance, and the power of friendship**. Their story served as a reminder that true connection knows no boundaries and that embracing diversity only enriches the tapestry of human existence.

In a world that can sometimes feel divided, Maya and Layla's friendship was a beacon of hope, showing that when we open our hearts to others and celebrate our differences, we create a more colorful and compassionate world for all.

Ram and Sham, on the contrary, have been the closest of friends, nearly inseparable since their childhood.

Ram had a knack for adventure and always pushed Sham out of his comfort zone, encouraging him to try new things. Conversely, Sham was more cautious and analytical, often playing the devil's advocate in their discussions.

Their dynamic friendship created the perfect environment for challenging each other's beliefs. Ram would introduce Sham to new perspectives and ideas that expanded his thinking, while Sham would question and scrutinize those ideas, leading to insightful debates that deepened their understanding of the world.

As they grew older, their social circle expanded to include diverse individuals with unique backgrounds and beliefs. Each interaction brought a new layer of understanding, shaping their perspectives in ways they never imagined. Ram and Sham's peer group became a melting pot of ideas, where differences were celebrated and curiosity was encouraged.

Through their interactions with various friends and social groups, Ram and Sham learned **the value of open-mindedness, empathy, and the power of diverse perspectives.**

The influence of their peer groups had a profound impact on their beliefs, shaping them into individuals who appreciated the beauty of diversity and the richness of human experiences.

Both stories demonstrate how crucial peer groups and social circles are in understanding the value of diversity and the depth of human experiences and establishing a strong belief system.

5. Crisis Moments:

Significant life events, such as a personal **crisis, illness, or loss, can lead to profound shifts in beliefs.** These events may prompt individuals to search for deeper meaning or question previously held convictions.

In times of crisis, our beliefs and perspectives can undergo significant transformation. These pivotal moments have the power to shake us to our core, forcing us to reassess our values, priorities, and understanding of the world around us.

When faced with personal disruptions, such as a health scare, the loss of a loved one, or a period of intense struggle, it is common to battle with existential questions and seek out a deeper sense of purpose.

These challenges can serve as catalysts for introspection and growth, pushing us to explore new avenues of thought and belief. While crisis moments can be incredibly difficult to navigate, they also have the potential to pave the way for personal evolution and the emergence of a more **resilient, compassionate, and enlightened self.**

Let's highlight The story of Rohan facing a personal financial crisis.

Rohan had always been a diligent and responsible individual when it came to managing his finances. However, a sudden turn of events left him facing a significant personal financial crisis. The company he had worked for over a decade unexpectedly downsized, leaving him without a job and struggling to make ends meet.

As he sat at his kitchen table, surrounded by bills and overdue notices, Rohan felt a wave of uncertainty wash over him. His once steadfast belief in financial stability was now shaken to its core. During this crisis, he found himself grappling with questions he had never considered before. What did money truly mean to him? How did he define success and security?

Despite the overwhelming challenges he faced, Rohan began to see this crisis as an opportunity for introspection and growth. He started to reassess his priorities, recognizing the importance of resilience, and adaptability, and seeking support from loved ones during tough times. Through this experience, Rohan discovered a newfound strength within himself and a deeper appreciation for the values that truly mattered in life.

Let's spotlight another story of a Rohit who has always been skeptical about the existence of a higher power and suddenly finds himself facing a serious illness.

Rohit's journey began like any other day, with the sun peeking through the curtains and birds chirping outside his window. He had always been a man of science, relying on logic and reason to navigate life's complexities. The concept of a higher power seemed like a distant, irrelevant idea to him.

However, fate had a different plan for Rohit. A sudden illness crept into his life, disrupting his routines and shattering his sense of invincibility. As he lay in his hospital bed, grappling with pain and uncertainty, a subtle shift began within him.

Days turned into weeks, and Rohit found himself pondering questions he had never considered before. The fragility of life, the mysteries of the universe, the possibility of a guiding force - these thoughts danced in his mind like elusive shadows.

Through the highs and lows of his recovery journey, Rohit discovered a newfound sense of humility and introspection. The once staunch skeptic found solace in moments of prayer and contemplation, seeking comfort in the unknown and finding strength in vulnerability.

As he emerged from the shadows of his illness, Rohit carried with him a deeper appreciation for the interconnectedness of life and the power of resilience. His journey from doubt to faith was not a linear path but a winding road of self-discovery and growth.

In the end, Rohit's story serves as a poignant reminder that even in the darkest of times, moments of crisis can spark transformation and lead us to unexpected revelations about ourselves and the world around us.

This shift in belief can be a profound and transformative experience, leading the person to explore new perspectives and contemplate deeper existential questions. It is during these crisis moments that individuals often discover inner resilience, faith, and a renewed sense of purpose that can guide them through their struggles and toward a path of healing and growth.

Similarly, the sudden loss of a loved one could lead someone to ponder the meaning of life and seek out philosophical or religious teachings for guidance. These pivotal moments have the power to challenge our perspectives and open our minds to new possibilities.

In times of profound loss, it is not uncommon to find solace in introspection and reflection. The experience of losing someone dear can catalyze deep contemplation and a reevaluation of our beliefs and values. It is during these moments of vulnerability that we may find ourselves drawn to seek comfort and understanding in spiritual or philosophical practices.

Let's delve into a poignant tale of a widow who tragically lost her son in an accident, her sole beloved family member.

In the wake of the devastating loss of her son, the widow found herself engulfed in a sea of grief and despair. Every corner of her home whispered memories of his laughter and warmth, now forever silenced. Yet, amidst the shadows of sorrow, a tiny flicker of resilience stirred within her heart.

As the days turned into weeks and the weeks into months, she found solace in the embrace of her community. They enveloped her in a blanket of support, each hug a gentle reminder that she was not alone in her pain. Slowly, the colors of life began to seep back into her world, muted but present.

In the quietude of her solitude, the widow embarked on a journey of self-discovery. She delved into literature that spoke of the human spirit's capacity to endure, to rise from the ashes of despair like a phoenix reborn. Through tear-stained pages and whispered prayers, she sought comfort in the wisdom of sages long gone, finding solace in their timeless words.

With each passing day, the widow's grief transformed into a beacon of hope. She etched her son's memory into the fabric of her being, a guiding light that illuminated her path forward. In the depths of her loss, she discovered a newfound strength, a resilience that echoed the whispers of generations before her.

And so, the widow, once shattered by sorrow, emerged from the crucible of her grief like a diamond forged under pressure. Her tale became a testament to the human spirit's capacity for healing and renewal, a reminder that even in the darkest of nights, the dawn of a new day awaits.

This individual's journey of **self-discovery** can often lead to profound insights and a newfound appreciation for the complexities of life. Embracing these moments of introspection and growth can ultimately help us find meaning and purpose in the face of adversity.

In summary, These stories serve as powerful reminders of the impact that crisis moments can have on our beliefs and perspectives. In the story of Rohan facing a personal financial crisis, we witness how challenges can lead to a reevaluation of priorities and a deeper search for meaning in life. Similarly, Rohit's journey from skepticism to facing a serious illness shows us how adversity can spark a profound shift in one's spiritual beliefs.

The poignant tale of the widow who tragically lost her son highlights the resilience of the human spirit in the face of unimaginable loss. Her story reminds us of the strength that can be found in moments of deep sorrow and how such experiences can shape our beliefs and values.

These narratives show us that in moments of crisis, **we can grow, evolve, and find new depths of understanding** about ourselves and the world around us. They underscore the importance of **compassion, empathy, and the capacity for renewal** even in the most challenging of circumstances.

6. Spirituality and Religion:

Many people derive their belief systems from religious or spiritual teachings. These systems often provide a framework for understanding the world, morality, and one's purpose in life.

For instance, many individuals look to their faith for guidance on how to navigate life's challenges and make decisions. Religious teachings can offer comfort in times of difficulty and serve as a source of strength and inspiration.

They also emphasize values such as compassion, forgiveness, and humility, which can shape how people interact with others and contribute to building a more harmonious society. Ultimately, whether through organized religion or personal spirituality, the beliefs that individuals hold can play a significant role in shaping their perspectives and guiding their actions.

The story of an old lady Monika Ji who believes in spirituality, the afterlife, and our place in the universe.

She often found herself drawn to moments of quiet contemplation, seeking solace in the beauty of nature and the mysteries of the cosmos. To her, the idea of spirituality was not just a belief system, but a deep connection to the energy that flowed through all living beings.

Her belief in the afterlife was rooted in a sense of comfort that there was something beyond this physical existence, a place where the soul could find peace and continue its journey. This belief gave her solace in times of loss and uncertainty, knowing that there was a greater plan at work.

As she gazed up at the stars in the night sky, she felt a profound sense of wonder and awe at the vastness of the universe. In those moments, she felt a deep connection to something greater than herself, a sense of belonging to a cosmic tapestry woven with threads of stardust and dreams.

Her beliefs were not just intellectual constructs but lived experiences that shaped how she interacted with the world around her. They gave her strength in times of adversity and inspired her to seek out the beauty and magic that surrounded her every day.

In a world that often seemed chaotic and unpredictable, her beliefs grounded her in a sense of purpose and meaning. They reminded her that she was part of something much larger than herself, a timeless dance of energy and spirit that connected all living things in a web of shared existence.

And so, she continued on her journey with an open heart and a curious mind, embracing the mysteries of life with a sense of wonder and gratitude for the beauty that surrounded her.

By embracing these shifts in beliefs, individuals can embark on a journey of **self-discovery and personal growth,** ultimately leading to a deeper understanding of themselves and the world around them.

Her story reveals the beauty of her unwavering faith and deep connection to the spiritual realm. Monika, an old lady, with wisdom etched in the lines of her face, shares tales of souls intertwined with the universe, of energies that transcend time and space. She speaks of a comforting afterlife, where love reigns supreme and peace knows no bounds.

As she weaves her stories, her eyes sparkle with a knowing gleam, inviting listeners to ponder the mysteries of existence. Through her words, she imparts the importance of kindness, compassion, and gratitude, teachings that resonate with the very essence of spirituality.

In her presence, one can't help but feel a sense of serenity and understanding, as if her beliefs have the power to soothe the restless soul and illuminate the path to inner harmony. Her story serves as a gentle reminder that, in a world filled with chaos and uncertainty, faith in something greater can provide solace and guidance.

As the old lady's voice fades into the hushed whispers of the wind, her message lingers in the hearts of those who have listened, a beacon of light in the darkness, a testament to the enduring power of spirituality and the boundless nature of the human spirit.

7. Philosophical Exploration:

Some individuals actively engage in philosophical inquiry to create or refine their belief systems. They may explore various philosophical traditions and build their own set of principles.

For instance, they might delve into ancient schools of thought like Stoicism or Taoism, seeking wisdom and guidance on how to navigate the complexities of life.

By studying these different philosophies, individuals can gain new perspectives and insights that help them make sense of the world around them.

Let's sport light a story of Samprada, who strongly believes in Philosophical Exploration and its transformative power.

Samprada, a dedicated seeker of truth, spent countless hours delving into the works of ancient philosophers, pondering the mysteries of existence, and questioning the very nature of reality.

Through her philosophical exploration, Samprada discovered a profound sense of interconnectedness with the world around her. She realized that every thought, action, and belief held a ripple effect that resonated far beyond herself.

As she continued her journey of introspection and contemplation, Samprada's perspective on life shifted. She began to see beauty in the complexities of existence and found solace in the uncertainties that once troubled him.

In embracing **Philosophical Exploration** as a way of life, Samprada not only expanded his intellectual horizons but also cultivated a deep sense of empathy and understanding towards others. His interactions were imbued with a newfound sense of compassion and wisdom that inspired those around her.

Through her unwavering commitment to philosophical inquiry, Samprada embodied the essence of a true seeker—one who navigates the depths of thought with humility, curiosity, and an open heart. In her pursuit of truth and enlightenment, Samprada found a profound sense of purpose and fulfillment that resonated with the very core of her being.

Ultimately, the process of philosophical inquiry can lead to personal growth and a deeper understanding of one's values and beliefs. It is a journey of self-discovery that allows individuals to cultivate a more profound connection with themselves and the universe.

8. Cultural and Societal Changes:

Shifts in society, cultural norms, and global events can influence how individuals view the world and shape their beliefs.

For instance, changes in societal attitudes toward issues like equality or environmentalism can impact personal beliefs. When we witness progress toward a more inclusive and sustainable world, it can inspire us to reevaluate our values and principles.

By staying open to new ideas and engaging in thoughtful discussions, we can continue to grow and adapt alongside our ever-changing society. Embracing these changes can lead to a greater sense of empathy, understanding, and connection with the world around us.

Exploring Cultural and Societal Changes: A Narrative of Mutual Respect and Understanding

The rise of the digital age has revolutionized the way people communicate and access information, leading to a more interconnected and fast-paced world. With the advent of social media platforms and instant messaging services, individuals are now able to connect with others from different corners of the globe in an instant. This has not only expanded their worldview but also exposed them to diverse perspectives and cultures they may not have encountered otherwise.

Moreover, global events such as the COVID-19 pandemic have highlighted the importance of solidarity and empathy among individuals worldwide. The shared experience of facing a common threat has brought people together, transcending geographical boundaries and fostering a sense of unity and compassion.

As a result, many individuals have reevaluated their priorities and values, recognizing the significance of human connection and collective well-being. In this constantly evolving landscape, individuals must remain open-minded, adaptable, and empathetic towards others.

By embracing diversity and understanding the various factors that shape people's beliefs and perspectives, individuals can foster a more inclusive and harmonious society built on mutual respect and understanding.

9. Self-Reflection and Introspection:

Deliberate self-reflection and introspection can help individuals clarify their values, priorities, and beliefs. Engaging in self-reflection and introspection allows individuals to **delve deep into their thoughts and emotions, gaining a better understanding of themselves.**

By taking the time to reflect on past experiences, beliefs, and actions, one can identify patterns, strengths, and areas for growth.

Let's dive into Niharika's tale of self-reflection and introspection, exploring her conflicting thoughts and feelings toward her loving mother.

Niharika sat by the window, a gentle breeze rustling the curtains as she delved into her thoughts. Memories of her childhood flooded back, each one intertwined with feelings of love, admiration, and sometimes frustration toward her mother. She pondered the times her mother's unwavering support had lifted her, contrasted with moments when she felt misunderstood and unheard.

As she reflected on these experiences, Niharika began to unravel the complexities of her relationship with her mother. She realized that her conflicting emotions were a natural part of their bond, shaped by shared experiences and individual perspectives. Through introspection, she acknowledged her growth and the importance of open communication in nurturing their connection.

In embracing self-reflection, Niharika discovered a newfound appreciation for the depth and resilience of her relationship with her mother. She recognized the power of understanding and empathy in navigating the intricacies of human connections, paving the way for deeper bonds and mutual growth.

Take another example of Self-reflection and introspection: Consider a scenario where an individual firmly believes in the saying "prevention is better than cure."

In various aspects of life, from health to finance, relationships to work, the individual's belief in the importance of prevention guides their decisions and actions.

They prioritize regular health check-ups, maintain emergency savings, invest in strong foundations for relationships, and implement risk management strategies in their work.

This proactive approach not only aligns with their belief but also helps create a sense of security and preparedness in the face of uncertainties.

As they navigate through life guided by the principle of prevention, they are likely to reinforce their belief even further through the positive outcomes and peace of mind it brings.

This process of Self-Reflection and Introspection can lead to greater self-awareness and personal development. Through introspection, individuals can align their values with their actions, set meaningful goals, and make decisions that are in line with their authentic selves. It is a powerful tool for self-improvement and cultivating a more fulfilling life.

Journaling, meditation, and therapy are tools that aid this process.

10. Synthesis and Integration:

Over time, individuals often synthesize their experiences, knowledge, and beliefs into a cohesive belief system. This system serves as a guiding framework for their **decisions, actions, and moral code.**

As these individuals navigate through life's myriad experiences and challenges, they gradually weave together a tapestry of wisdom and insight. This intricate web of beliefs and values not only shapes their perspective but also influences the way they interact with the world around them.

Through the process of synthesis, they blend their truths with external influences, creating a unique combination of ideas that form the foundation of their belief system.

This integration of diverse perspectives allows for a more sophisticated understanding of the complexities of life and fosters empathy and compassion toward others.

Embark on the tale of Synthesis and Integration: Follow Nickel's story as he forbids his well-educated wife from seeking employment outside the household.

He firmly believes that women are the backbone of their families. Only, A well-educated mother can provide better care for her children. As Nickel navigates the complexities of balancing tradition and modernity in his family, he begins to realize that true strength lies in mutual respect and support between partners.

Through open communication and understanding, Nickel and his wife embark on a journey of growth and empowerment, challenging societal norms and embracing the idea that true equality and fulfillment come from valuing each other's aspirations and contributions.

Their story serves as a reminder that while individual beliefs and values are important, true harmony and progress can be achieved through a shared vision built on **compassion, respect, and unity.**

Thus, the ongoing journey of synthesis and integration not only enriches their individual growth but also enables them to contribute positively to the collective tapestry of humanity.

As they navigate life, these principles act as a compass, helping them make choices aligned with their core values and guiding them through the calm waters and stormy seas of existence.

This belief system not only shapes their identity but also influences how they engage with the world around them, fostering a sense of connection and purpose, providing direction, and grounding their decisions and actions in a moral framework that reflects their core values and principles.

11. Openness to Change:

The ability to remain open to new information and perspectives is essential for evolving one's beliefs. Being willing to adapt and revise beliefs when warranted is a sign of intellectual flexibility.

Embracing the concept of openness to change allows individuals to grow and learn constantly. By staying receptive to new ideas and different viewpoints, people can expand their knowledge and evolve their understanding of the world around them.

This willingness to adapt and update beliefs based on new information is a testament to one's intellectual curiosity and capacity for growth. It is through this continuous process of learning and reevaluation that individuals can truly develop a comprehensive and sophisticated understanding of the complexities of life.

So, remember, staying open to change is not a sign of weakness, but rather a demonstration of strength and a commitment to personal development.

For instance, consider the scenario of a person who has held a certain belief for years. If new evidence emerges that contradicts this belief, the intellectually flexible person will be open to re-evaluating their stance.

This doesn't necessarily mean they will abandon their belief altogether, but they will be willing to consider alternative viewpoints and adjust their thinking accordingly.

Conversely, a person who is unwilling to revise their beliefs in light of new information may become closed-minded and stagnant in their thinking.

Let's embark on the journey of Grandmother Rossy and how her ready-to-learn attitude helped her.

The grandmother lacked the modern traits to overcome her grandchildren's growing mentalities. The remarkable journey of Grandma Rossy, a woman whose wisdom was as vast as her love for her family.

As her grandchildren blossomed into young individuals with evolving perspectives and fresh ideas, Grandma Rossy found herself facing a new challenge. The world around her was changing rapidly, and she realized that to connect with her grandchildren and understand their growing mentalities, she needed to embrace openness to change.

With a heart full of love and a mind ready to learn, Grandma Rossy embarked on a journey of self-discovery and growth. She sought to understand the new trends, technologies, and beliefs that shaped her grandchildren's world. Through patient conversations, shared experiences, and a genuine curiosity for the unknown, Grandma Rossy began to bridge the gap between generations.

As she listened to her grandchildren's stories and shared her wisdom, Grandma Rossy discovered that true intellectual flexibility lies not in rigid beliefs, but in the willingness to explore new perspectives and ideas. With each passing day, she learned to appreciate the beauty of change and the richness it brought to her relationships with her grandchildren.

In the end, Grandma Rossy's openness to change not only strengthened her bond with her family but also enriched her own life in ways she never imagined. And so, this overwhelming story teaches us that the willingness to evolve and embrace new ways of thinking is a gift that knows no age – for in the journey of learning, we find the true essence of growth and connection.

Intellectual flexibility is therefore a valuable trait that can lead to personal growth and a deeper understanding of the world around us.

12. Personal Growth:

Belief systems can evolve as individuals undergo personal growth and self-improvement journeys. This growth may lead to a deeper understanding of oneself and the world.

For instance, consider a scenario, where someone who once held rigid beliefs about success being solely defined by material wealth, begins to prioritize personal fulfillment and emotional well-being instead.

This shift in perspective can be a transformative experience, opening up new possibilities and fostering a greater sense of inner peace and contentment.

The Tale of Emma, Who Devoted Herself to Raising Her Children and Fulfilling Her Inner Thirst for Knowledge: Embracing Motherhood and Personal Growth

Emma had a good education and focused on raising her children after delivering twins. Despite her commitment to her kids, she remained dedicated to continuous learning for her personal growth.

Emma, with her unwavering dedication to her children, found joy in every moment spent nurturing and guiding them. She believed that education was not limited to textbooks but also encompassed the valuable life lessons she could impart to her little ones.

As she watched her twins grow and flourish under her care, Emma's heart swelled with pride and love. She instilled in them the importance of kindness, empathy, and perseverance, knowing that these qualities would serve them well in their journeys ahead. Emma's home was filled with laughter, love, and the sweet chaos of childhood, a testament to her unyielding commitment to motherhood.

In the quiet moments when her children slept, she would steal a few precious minutes to feed her thirst for knowledge, relishing the opportunity to expand her horizons and deepen her understanding of the world.

Emma's journey into motherhood was a profound one, filled with both challenges and joys. She approached each day with unwavering love and patience, setting a beautiful example for her children. Her dedication to their well-being was unwavering, as she strived to create a nurturing and supportive environment for them to thrive in.

Despite the demands of motherhood, Emma also understood the importance of self-care and personal development. She made time for her interests and hobbies, all while instilling in her children the value of lifelong learning and growth. Through her actions, Emma showed that being a devoted mother didn't mean sacrificing one's dreams and aspirations.

As her children grew, Emma's bond with them only strengthened. She shared with them the wonders of the world, teaching them valuable life lessons and encouraging them to pursue their passions. Emma's story became a testament to the power of love, resilience, and the incredible journey of motherhood.

Emma's story was not just about raising children; it was a tale of strength, resilience, the incredible journey of motherhood, and the enduring power of a mother's love.

This journey of self-discovery and personal growth is a powerful testament to the resilience and capacity for change that resides within each of us.

In Topic Conclusion

As individuals continue to learn, reflect, and evolve, their belief systems can adapt and expand, allowing for a more holistic and balanced approach to navigating life's challenges and joys.

By embracing this evolution of belief systems, individuals can cultivate a more authentic and fulfilling existence, rooted in compassion, empathy, and a deeper connection to themselves and the world around them.

It's important to note that belief systems vary widely from person to person. Some individuals may have rigid and unchanging beliefs, while others maintain more flexible and adaptable belief systems.

The process of belief evolution and creation is ongoing and unique to each individual, reflecting their life experiences and personal values.

III. Practicing "The Art of Believing".

"The Art of Believing" is a fundamental concept that emphasizes the significance of positive thinking and beliefs in achieving success and fulfilling one's goals and aspirations.

It could be pursuing a fulfilling career that brings joy and satisfaction, traveling to new and exciting destinations around the world, fostering meaningful relationships with loved ones and friends, making a positive impact on the community through volunteering and activism, continuously learning and growing to become the best version of oneself.

Practicing this art involves cultivating a mindset that embraces positive thoughts and unwavering faith in oneself and one's abilities, others, and particularly in the divine.

A. Common Areas to Practice "The Art of Believing" in Everyday Life

1. Self-belief

Practicing **"The Art of Believing"** begins with **believing in self.** This involves trusting in self-abilities, having confidence in self-decisions, and maintaining a positive self-image.

For instance, By recognizing personal strengths and weaknesses, individuals can concentrate on embracing their strengths and enhancing areas that require development.

This self-awareness can lead to better decision-making, more effective communication, and increased productivity. It also allows individuals to recognize when to seek help or delegate tasks to others who may be stronger in certain areas.

Furthermore, acknowledging one's limitations can prevent burnout and promote a healthy life balance. Overall, self-awareness and self-belief are valuable tools for personal growth and success.

Eventually, by practicing **"The Art of Believing"**, individuals can be ready to face any situation and circumstances as they know their abilities, strengths, and weaknesses.

A Story of Self-Belief- A Journey From Hope to Healing.

Let's Embark on My Journey, I Chose Self-Healing Over Surgery- A Journey from Rescued to Restoration.

I would like to share one of my **"Self-Belief Faith-Healing"** stories. In the year 2018, I experienced an accident that resulted in the dislocation of my elbow. Upon reaching the nearest hospital, I was informed by the orthopedic doctor that immediate surgery was necessary to correct the torn ligaments – medial collateral ligament, lateral collateral ligament, and annular ligament – to restore elbow stability.

At that time, I was losing my sensation and consciousness, as I had terrible pain, a swollen and dislocated elbow, ruptured ligaments, blood vessels, and nerve supply. At the same time, I was alone, my husband was out of the station, my 5-year-old daughter was in school, and my neighbors took me to the hospital. I was unable to decide at that moment, to go for immediate surgery.

This had all been assessed by the Doctor, At that time he just wanted me to escape the danger and relax from the terrible situation. He repositioned my dislocated elbow bone and secured it with a cast to alleviate discomfort. He was also prescribed analgesic medication to manage the pain. At this point, surgery was on hold.

My medical knowledge and belief in my self-healing power, made me question whether surgery is the only necessary option. Is it possible for my body's natural healing abilities to cure me and for me to gain elbow stability once again? As I knew that the blood supply was very low in ligaments the healing process could be deadly, and the three-sided ligament was torn so immediate surgery was needed. I was in a big dilemma. Should I go for self-healing or a medical procedural surgery?

However, after much contemplation, I felt an inner calling to believe in my body’s innate power: Self-healing. “I Chose Self-Healing Over Medical Procedural Surgery.”

My husband and family members were not initially on board with my decision to forgo surgery, as they were understandably concerned for my well-being. We sought out multiple opinions from orthopedic doctors and physiotherapists, who all recommended surgery.

The decision was a difficult one, as I believed in myself and my body’s innate power to heal and restore the elbow stability. I struggled to convey my inner feelings to my loved ones. Ultimately, I decided to trust my inner voice and undergo a self-healing process with the help of an orthopedic doctor who was willing to work with me.

The journey was not an easy one. It was a challenging journey, but after three months of treatment and physiotherapy, my elbow recovered and healed completely, and was stable once again. Throughout the healing process, I remained focused on my end goal and trusted in my higher-self for the self-healing process and the doctor's actions.

With dedication and perseverance, I pushed through the difficult moments, always keeping my eye on the light at the end of the tunnel. Each physiotherapy session was a step forward, a reminder that progress was being made, even if it was slow. I learned the importance of patience and self-care, understanding that healing takes time and cannot be rushed. As my elbow grew stronger, so did my belief in the power of resilience and faith in the body's ability to heal itself.

The experience taught me valuable lessons about the mind-body connection and the importance of trust in the healing journey, the power of self-belief, and the importance of listening to one's inner voice. It demonstrated to me that having faith in self-abilities and the body's natural healing powers can result in a remarkable recovery.

When we listen to our inner voice, we establish a connection with our authentic selves. This enables us to pursue our dreams and aspirations, leading us towards our goals and accomplishments.

Embracing self-belief and listening to our inner voice can empower us to overcome challenges, take risks, and ultimately achieve success. Trusting in ourselves is a powerful tool that can propel us forward on our journey toward fulfillment and happiness.

This narrative is a poignant reminder of the transformative power of self-belief and the remarkable resilience that lies within each of us. It highlights the importance of advocating for oneself, trusting in the body's natural healing processes, and embracing the journey towards self-restoration.

My message for others is simple - trust in yourself, believe in your body's ability to heal, and never underestimate the power of your determination. Remember, you are stronger than you think, and with perseverance and self-belief, you can overcome any obstacle that comes your way.

2. In Relationships:

Believing in the potential and goodness of others is crucial for nurturing healthy and fulfilling relationships. This includes believing in their abilities, supporting their dreams, and maintaining trust and confidence in them.

For instance, We all know that spending time with someone allows us to better understand their strengths and weaknesses. When it comes to supporting those close to us, it's essential to encourage their strengths, listen to their concerns, stand with them during their tough times, and provide empathy. By taking a positive approach, we can help to eliminate weaknesses and bring out the best in each other.

Believing in someone's potential also means recognizing their unique qualities and talents. Rather than trying to change them to fit a certain mold, we should embrace their individuality and encourage them to pursue their passions. This can lead to a deeper level of trust and respect in the relationship, as we show that we value and appreciate who they truly are.

Maintaining trust and confidence is another important aspect of nurturing healthy relationships. This means being honest and transparent with one another and respecting each other's boundaries. When conflicts arise, it's important to communicate openly and respectfully and work together toward a solution that benefits both parties/sides.

Overall, nurturing healthy and fulfilling relationships requires a combination of belief in each other's potential, support and encouragement, trust and confidence, and open communication. By prioritizing these values, we can build strong and meaningful connections with those around us.

Let's spotlight the journey of Andrew Thomas and How he devoted his wife to achieve her dream project.- A Journey, True meaning of Relationship. From Nothing to Everything.

Rachel, who was highly educated, aimed to set up a wellness center. Despite objections from her in-laws and facing financial difficulties, her husband Andrew stood by her decision.

Andrew's unwavering support was the cornerstone of Rachel's success. With his reassurance and belief in her vision, Rachel was able to navigate through the challenges that came her way. Together, they tackled each obstacle hand in hand, turning setbacks into stepping stones towards their shared goal.

Andrew not only provided emotional support but also practical assistance, helping Rachel with research, planning, and connecting with potential investors. His encouragement and dedication were the fuel that kept Rachel motivated during moments of doubt. With Andrew by her side, Rachel's dream of establishing a wellness center started to materialize, bringing them closer together as a team.

Their journey was a testament to the power of love, unity, trust, faith in each other, and unwavering support in turning dreams into reality.

As Rachel's wellness center flourished, Andrew's pride and joy knew no bounds, knowing that he had played a crucial role in making his wife's dream come true. Their story serves as an inspiration to all, highlighting the strength of a partnership built on mutual respect, support, and shared dreams.

Their journey together was not without challenges, but they faced each obstacle hand in hand, emerging stronger each time. Rachel's creativity and dedication, combined with Andrew's unwavering encouragement and business acumen, created a harmonious balance that propelled their wellness center to success.

Their shared vision and commitment to each other not only strengthened their bond but also became a beacon of hope for others pursuing their passions. Through their perseverance and unity, they proved that with love and collaboration, any dream is achievable.

As Rachel's clients raved about the nurturing environment she had created, and Andrew beamed with pride at her accomplishments, it was clear that their partnership was truly a force to be reckoned with. Together, they showed the world the power of teamwork, love, and unwavering support in turning dreams into reality.

3. On Career and Goals:

Believing in your career path, your abilities, and your goals is essential for achieving success. It involves visualizing success, maintaining a positive mindset, and having faith in your skills and capabilities.

For instance, envision yourself as a confident and skilled professional in your field. Picture yourself excelling in your work, overcoming challenges with grace, and achieving your goals with determination.

By maintaining a positive mindset, you can attract opportunities, stay motivated during tough times, and navigate obstacles with resilience. Have faith in your skills and capabilities by continuously honing them, seeking growth opportunities, and believing in your potential to succeed.

Remember, success is not just about reaching your goals, but also about the journey of growth, learning, and self-discovery along the way. Stay committed, stay focused, and trust in yourself to turn your aspirations into reality.

For instance: Let's say you want to become a successful writer.

Believing in yourself would mean envisioning yourself as a published author, visualizing your book on shelves in bookstores, and imagining readers enjoying your work. It also means maintaining a positive attitude and outlook, even when faced with rejection or setbacks.

Remember, every successful writer faced rejection at some point, but they persevered because they believed in their abilities and their passion for writing. Having faith in your skills and capabilities means trusting that you have the talent, drive, and determination to achieve your goals.

"It means taking risks, putting in the hard work, and never giving up on yourself."

By believing in yourself and your career path, you can overcome obstacles, achieve success, and live the life you've always dreamed of.

A Journey From Booklet to Bookstore: My Writing Adventure

I have harbored a desire to write a book since I was 21 years old. I would always carry a piece of paper, whether it was fresh paper or a tissue, and start writing wherever I found myself – be it a coffee table, dining table, library, classroom, or even on a college bus. My friends would always spot me writing, no matter where or when.

However, my acquired knowledge and skills have not been sufficient to make it happen. I was Gradually but consistently honing my writing skills, with the hope that one day my work would be acknowledged.

To start with my writing journey as a humble writer with a passion for storytelling and a dream of sharing my words with the world. Armed with determination and a love for crafting narratives, I embarked on my writing adventure, in 2020, by creating a 40 to 50-page booklet filled with my thoughts and ideas, focusing on health topics like preventive measures against illnesses, diabetes and hypertension awareness, the power of belief, and so forth.

Each page was a canvas for my imagination, and with every word I penned, I felt a sense of fulfillment and purpose. I shared the booklet with my close circle, including colleagues, friends, and family members, who appreciated my writing skills.

As time went on, the positive feedback and encouragement from my loved ones fueled my passion for writing even more. Gradually and consistently my confidence grew, and my writing skills sharpened. After multiple attempts, I decided to expand my horizons and delve deeper into the world of storytelling. With newfound determination, I diligently crafted my ideas and thoughts into a full-fledged book.

The turning point in my writing journey came when I decided to approach publishers and share my work with the world. I have chosen to write a book about belief and its impact on life's journey.

This book, **"The Art of Believing,"** was my first endeavor. Crafting a book focused on belief was a significant undertaking for me, as I strongly believe that an individual's beliefs influence the life they aspire to have. I wrote this book with the aspiration that everyone can lead a peaceful life, free from suffering, pain, and illness through the practice of believing.

The process was not easy and without its challenges, but with my perseverance and unwavering dedication, I transformed my humble booklet into a manuscript filled with heart and soul in each piece, I honed my craft and polished my words until they shone brightly on the page, through hectic days, late nights, and numerous hours of writing, editing, and rewriting.

After months of perseverance, unwavering dedication, and steadfast long-term faith in my story, I have finally finished writing my first book. From this moment on, my writing adventure reached a new chapter. With the support of my readers and the unwavering belief in the power of storytelling, I know this is only the beginning of an exciting journey ahead. There is still a long way to go, I plan to write more books with fresh and innovative ideas on various aspects of life.

The journey from a simple booklet to a published book was a testament to the power of believing in self, staying true to self-passion, and never giving up on your long-term goals and dreams.

Ultimately, my writing adventure taught me that success is not just about reaching the destination but also about embracing the journey with all its ups and downs. It is about having the courage to chase your long-term goals and dreams, the resilience to overcome obstacles, and the faith to keep moving forward, staying motivated to fuel your inner core, in one word at a time.

Remember that your belief in yourself is a powerful tool that can propel you towards your aspirations. Stay focused, keep pushing forward, and trust in your journey. The path to success may have challenges, but with unwavering belief in yourself, you can overcome any obstacles that come your way. Trust in your abilities and keep striving for your dreams - they are closer than you think.

My message to the other writers: Keep writing, keep dreaming, and keep believing in yourself. Your journey may have challenges, but each word you write is a step closer to your dream becoming a reality.

Embrace the process, learn from setbacks, and celebrate every small victory along the way. Your story matters, your voice is unique, and the world is waiting to hear what you have to say. So, pick up your pen, let your creativity flow, and remember that your persistence and passion will guide you toward achieving your goals. Keep writing and never underestimate the power of your words.

4. Health and well-being:

Believing in your ability to maintain good health and well-being is important for leading a balanced and fulfilling life.

This includes having faith in your body's ability to heal by yourself and regenerate, believing in the power of self-healing, and self-care practices, and maintaining a positive outlook on your overall well-being.

Let’s Explore the body's innate power of Self-healing: 3Rs- Repair, Regenerate, and Restore

Self-healing power is a remarkable ability that resides within each one of us. It is the innate capacity of our bodies to repair, regenerate, and restore balance to maintain overall health and well-being.

When we embrace practices that support our self-healing abilities, such as proper nutrition, regular exercise, mindfulness, and stress-management techniques, we empower our bodies to function at their optimal level.

By listening to our bodies, honoring their needs, and providing them with the care they deserve, we can tap into this incredible self-healing power and enhance our quality of life.

Embracing a holistic approach to wellness that nurtures the mind, body, and spirit is key to unlocking the full potential of our self-healing abilities. By believing in the wisdom of your body and allowing it to guide you on a path towards greater Vitality. Instead of relying on medication and costly hospital investigations, we can trust in our innate healing abilities that lie within us.

By adopting a mindset that embraces the power of our bodies to heal, we open the door to a more holistic approach to wellness. This shift in perspective encourages us to explore alternative methods such as meditation, yoga, mindful eating, and other practices that support our body's natural healing processes.

Just think about how amazing it is that a simple cut on our hand can heal within a day or two, or how our bones can mend themselves after being fractured. Our bodies are truly remarkable and by trusting in their ability to heal, we can embrace a holistic approach to health and well-being.

Additionally, it empowers us to take an active role in our health journey, promoting a deeper connection with ourselves and a greater sense of control over our well-being.

Embracing the belief in our body's innate ability to heal not only enhances our physical health but also nurtures our mental and emotional wellness, creating a harmonious balance that can lead to a more fulfilling and vibrant life.

Let's Embrace the Self-Healing Story:

A Journey From Hilarious to Healing: My Self-Healing Story of Pregnancy-Induced Complications.

Pregnancy is often perceived as a joyous and exciting time, filled with anticipation and hope. However, when faced with unexpected complications such as pregnancy-induced diabetes. The journey can become challenging. In sharing my personal experience, I hope to offer a beacon of light and hope to others navigating the path of pregnancy-induced complications.

A Twist in the Journey We were very Joyful and excited about discovering the pregnancy. Everything went very well till the second trimester. At the beginning of the third trimester, we showed a sudden rise in blood sugar levels on routine blood investigations. We were horrified and concerned when diagnosed by a Gynecologist with pregnancy-induced diabetes. Felt overwhelmed and anxious about the implications for both myself and the growing baby.

Dealing with the Diagnosis My medical knowledge helped me navigate more about pregnancy-induced diabetes and its potential risks. I believed in approaching a body's innate ability to heal and Restore. I adopted a new lifestyle by making dietary changes, incorporating more fresh vegetables and fruits, transitioning to a vegetarian diet, and integrating yoga, prayers, and meditation into my routine. I monitored my blood sugar levels regularly, attended routine natal checkups with my healthcare provider, connected with support groups, and consulted professionals who specialize in gestational diabetes. This approach helped me manage pregnancy-induced complications without the need for medication.

Unleashing the Power of Positivity I found solace in the power of a positive mindset and the impact it had on managing pregnancy-induced complications. Cultivated gratitude and focused on the blessings of motherhood. Embraced daily Prayers, affirmations, and visualization techniques helped me to stay motivated and centered.

A Positive Birth Experience, Sharing the story of a successful birth experience despite the challenges caused by pregnancy-induced diabetes, I Celebrated the resilience and strength exhibited during labor, I was overwhelmed and joyful, finally meeting my baby, and the fulfillment of becoming a mother.

Hope and Healing, Pregnancy-induced complications may present unexpected hurdles, but through embracing practices that support self-healing abilities, medical knowledge, Professional team support, a positive mindset, prayers, meditation, and positive affirmations it is possible to navigate through this journey with grace and optimism.

My story serves as a testament to the power of healing, highlighting the importance of self-care, support, and embracing the miracles that can arise from adversity. May it inspire others to find strength and hope in their healing journeys.

My message on self-healing for others: My perspective on self-healing emphasizes the remarkable ability of the body to **repair, regenerate, and rejuvenate.** Instead of frequent hospital visits, costly investigations, and relying on medications, it's essential to harness the body's natural healing capacity. Making thoughtful choices to prioritize the body's self-healing process is key to overall well-being.

Remember, Never underestimate the body's innate power to heal, cure, and transform itself.

5. Personal growth, and mindset:

Practicing the art of believing involves having a growth mindset and believing in your ability to "**Learn, Adapt, and Grow.**" This includes believing in your potential to overcome challenges, embracing failures as learning opportunities, and continuously striving for personal growth.

For instance, if you're faced with a difficult task at work, in your professional life, or in your personal life, instead of immediately feeling overwhelmed and defeated, you can approach the situation with a growth mindset.

This means recognizing that you may not have all the answers right away, but that you can learn and improve over time. You can break the task down into smaller, more manageable steps and focus on making progress one step at a time.

By believing in your ability to overcome challenges and grow, you can approach any situation with confidence and resilience. This mindset can also help you embrace failures as opportunities for growth and learning, rather than seeing them as setbacks.

Let's Embark on a Journey with Vijaya Rapaka, a Young Lady, and How She Used the Transformative Power of a Growth Mindset- From Learn and Adopt to Grow.

She began her career abroad at 19, far from her family. Initially, she felt isolated, insecure, and anxious in a new environment, worrying about work pressure. At times, she felt overwhelmed and contemplated quitting her job.

She constantly wanted for her return home, pondering over her family, children, spouse, and dear ones. Amidst the multitude of thoughts racing through her mind, she often felt overwhelmed and contemplated leaving her job and escaping the circumstances that engulfed her.

On the contrary, she pondered the valuable opportunity to work abroad, reflecting on the effort and money invested in the overseas venture. With a promising future in sight, she envisioned offering her children the finest education and quality of life. If she decided to resign, she would have to face all the repercussions. She was in a big battle to make the right decision and was torn between choosing to leave or persevere.

She slowly but steadily conquered her mental exhaustion from overthinking, fears, and concerns about leaving her job. In just a few months, she successfully changed her mindset and began to adopt the belief in the transformative potential of a growth mindset – **to learn, adapt, and grow – to overcome her inner conflicts.**

After making the correct decision, the Universe stood ready to grant her every wish – quality education for her children and a comfortable life. Through her unwavering perseverance and positive mindset, she reached numerous milestones of success. She learned gradually and patiently from the situations and circumstances, adapting to new skills to thrive in her field and continually progress in her life.

After two decades of experience, she now provides opportunities for others to work abroad. Vijaya's journey was challenging; as a woman, she became an inspiration for others.

Vijaya's journey of growth and transformation serves as a beacon of inspiration for all who encounter obstacles and uncertainties in their lives. Through her perseverance and commitment to adopting a growth mindset, she not only overcame her initial fears and doubts but also flourished in her career and personal life.

Her story reminds us of the power that lies within us to **learn, adapt, and grow** from every experience. It teaches us that challenges are not roadblocks but stepping stones towards success. Vijaya's unwavering determination to push past her limitations and embrace change paved the way for a brighter future filled with opportunities and fulfillment.

As she continues to thrive and make a difference in the lives of others, Vijaya stands as a testament to the incredible strength and resilience that women possess. Her journey exemplifies the transformative impact of a growth mindset and serves as a reminder that with dedication and belief in oneself, anything is possible.

Ultimately, practicing the art of believing can lead to a more fulfilling and successful life, **both personally and professionally.**

6. Dreams and Aspirations:

Believing in your dreams and aspirations is crucial for turning them into reality. This involves visualizing and affirming your goals, having faith in your abilities to achieve them, and taking consistent action toward their fulfillment.

For instance: If you dream of becoming a successful entrepreneur, you must believe in yourself and your vision. Visualize yourself as a successful business owner, surrounded by happy employees and satisfied customers. Affirm your goals by repeating positive affirmations such as "I am capable of achieving my dreams" or "I have the skills and knowledge to succeed." Have faith in your abilities and trust that you can overcome any obstacles that may arise.

Ultimately, success is not just about dreaming but also about taking smart action by working hard every day. Set clear, actionable goals for yourself and create a plan to work towards them consistently.

Be disciplined in your efforts, stay dedicated to your vision, and persevere through any setbacks. With belief, positivity, resilience, and action, you can turn your dreams into reality.

From Dreaming to Daring: Let's spotlight the story of Raaj Murthy, a 23-year-old Aspiring Entrepreneur

Raaj Murthy, a nature enthusiast, had a special fondness for the ocean, which captivated him. Since the age of 15, he found solace in the ocean, feeling as though Mother Ocean had a message for him. With his school and college located near the ocean, he would often take breaks between classes to detach from the hectic school environment and immerse himself in the calming presence of the ocean. While others were engrossed in their studies, he would admire the beauty of the ocean through the windows.

He not only engaged in this routine, but he also devoted time to seaside walks twice daily, in the morning and evening. He conversed with nature, and wherever he ventured, the ocean seemed to accompany him. Almost every day, he spent numerous hours near the ocean.

At 21, he used to take evening strolls hand in hand with his girlfriend. She noticed his fascination with the ocean and how he always seemed to be searching for answers. His routine involved walking to college in the morning, from college to evening walks, and then back home. Soon time flew by, and as his college days neared their end, he finally found the last piece of the puzzle and understood what Mother Ocean had been trying to tell him.

He determined himself to establish a company that manufactures sea vehicles. Despite lacking family and financial backing, he was determined to succeed. Fresh out of college, he devised a plan to create a boat manufacturing business and had unwavering faith in his vision. To kickstart his venture, he approached a fisherman and requested to give him an unused or broken small fishing boat.

He acquired all the essential knowledge and commenced his training. With his old fishing boat, he approached the closest bank to request a loan. He set up a well-equipped manufacturing yard.

His Journey was not an easy one. He had a mixed experience, the rejections from banks, and felt difficulty setting up a manufacturing yard and a lot more. After six months of persistent dedication and faith in his vision, he successfully set sail with his newly built boat on the sea. Since then, he has continuously strived to reach new milestones. To achieve new milestones every time, he increases the difficulty level. He appreciates the beauty of Mother Nature and lives by the motto **"An Ocean of Memories."**

Finally, in 2004, By the local administration, he was recognized with the **"Young Entrepreneur"** award. He was grateful for his work and dedication, expressing gratitude to the divine and his faith. Since then, he has never wavered in his beliefs, using his faith to appreciate the beauty of life.

Raaj Murthy's inspiring journey serves as a testament to the strength of unwavering belief. Despite facing numerous challenges, his determination and faith in his vision propelled him forward. Through persistence and dedication, he turned his dream of a boat manufacturing business into reality, demonstrating the remarkable impact of belief on our ability to achieve our goals.

Just as Raaj's story illustrates, cultivating a mindset rooted in positivity and self-belief can lead us to overcome obstacles and reach new heights. Embracing the power of belief allows us to tap into our full potential and create the future we envision.

Raaj Murthy's journey serves as a testament to the power of dreams and aspirations. His unwavering belief in the message he felt the ocean whisper to him led him on a remarkable path of entrepreneurship. Despite facing challenges and setbacks, he remained resolute in his vision of manufacturing sea vehicles.

With determination and perseverance, Raaj overcame obstacles such as financial struggles and bank rejections. Through his dedication and faith, he turned his dream into a reality, launching his boat on the sea after months of hard work. His story is a reminder that with courage, persistence, and a clear vision, one can transform aspirations into tangible achievements.

As we reflect on Raaj's inspiring journey, let us remember that every dream pursued with passion and purpose has the potential to blossom into something extraordinary. May his story inspire us all to embrace our dreams, no matter how audacious they may seem, and to journey towards them with unwavering determination.

Message from Raaj Murthy, His belief is in saying these quotes: When life puts you in a tough situation, **"DON'T SAY WHY ME, SAY TRY ME".**

7. Resilience and Overcoming Adversity:

Practicing the art of believing includes believing in your resilience and ability to overcome obstacles and adversity.

This involves maintaining a positive attitude, trusting that challenges are opportunities in disguise, and having faith in your ability to bounce back from setbacks.

For instance, if you're faced with a difficult situation at work, instead of dwelling on the negative aspects, try to focus on the opportunities for growth and learning that may arise from the experience.

This shift in mindset can help you stay motivated and continue to work towards your goals, even in the face of adversity. It's important to remember that setbacks are a natural part of the learning process and that each challenge you overcome will help you build your resilience and confidence for the next one.

So, keep believing in yourself and your ability to overcome obstacles, and you'll be well on your way to achieving your goals and dreams.

A Story of Resilience and Overcoming Adversity: Abraham and His Fighting with Adversity

Abraham completed engineering and was waiting for a job. He decided to focus on improving his skills while waiting for the right opportunity to come along. He dedicated his time to learning new technologies, networking with professionals in his field, and volunteering his expertise to help others.

Despite facing rejection and uncertainty, he remained determined and optimistic, knowing that his hard work and perseverance would eventually pay off. Each day, he reminded himself that setbacks were just stepping stones to success and that every challenge he encountered only made him stronger and more prepared for the future.

Finally, after a year of dedication and hard work, Abraham received a job offer from a prestigious company that recognized his resilience and determination.

This experience taught him the valuable lesson that belief in self and the willingness to overcome adversity are key ingredients for achieving success in any endeavor. As he embarked on this new chapter in his career, Abraham carried with him the lessons learned during his struggles.

He knew that self-belief and perseverance were not just qualities to possess but the very foundation upon which success is built. And with this newfound wisdom, he was ready to face whatever challenges lay ahead, confident in his ability to conquer them all.

He set an example for others around him, inspiring them with his unwavering determination and resilience. Abraham's story became a beacon of hope for those facing their own battles, showing that with courage and a positive mindset, one can overcome even the most daunting of obstacles.

His journey was not without its setbacks, but each stumble only served to strengthen his resolve. Every defeat was met with a renewed sense of determination, driving him to push harder and reach further than before. Abraham's unwavering spirit and refusal to give up in the face of adversity inspired many to believe in their own potential and strive for greatness.

Through his dedication and unwavering faith in himself, Abraham proved that with perseverance and a never-say-die attitude, anything is possible. His story serves as a reminder that no matter how tough the road may seem, resilience and a positive outlook can pave the way to triumph over adversity.

8. Spirituality and Faith:

Believing in something greater than oneself, whether it be a higher power, the universe, or the creator of life, can provide a sense of purpose and guidance. This involves nurturing spiritual practices, having faith in the divine, and maintaining a sense of belief in the unseen forces at work in the universe.

For instance, many people find comfort in prayer or meditation, which can help them connect with their inner selves and the divine. Others may find solace in practicing yoga or attending religious services, which can provide a sense of community and support.

In addition to providing a sense of purpose and guidance, belief in something greater than oneself can also help individuals navigate difficult times in their lives. When faced with challenges or adversity, having faith in the divine can offer a source of strength and hope. It can provide a sense of comfort and assurance that everything happens for a reason or a purpose and that there is a higher power at work.

Ultimately, believing in something greater than oneself can bring a sense of peace and fulfillment to one's life. It can provide a sense of meaning and direction, and help individuals live their lives with intention and purpose.

Whether it is through spiritual practices, religious beliefs, or a connection to the universe, embracing a belief in something greater can bring a sense of unity and connection to all of humanity.

The story of Mr. Raaj Demonstrates How Spirituality Can Serve as a Guiding Light During Difficult Times, Illuminating The Path to Healing and Transformation.

A young man who discovered comfort in his faith during a challenging period in his life, when he encountered a medical problem. He restored his vision and turned to his religious beliefs for guidance and comfort. Through prayer and meditation, Mr. Raaj gained the strength and clarity needed to overcome his obstacles.

During his deepest struggles, Mr. Raaj found solace in the teachings of religious beliefs and spiritual traditions. Through introspection and meditation/prayer, he began to unravel the tangled emotions within him, finding clarity and peace in the stillness of his mind.

As he delved deeper into his spiritual journey, Mr. Raaj discovered the profound wisdom that lay hidden in the depths of his soul. With each passing day, he embraced the power of forgiveness, compassion, and self-love, paving the way for his healing and transformation.

Through the gentle whispers of his inner voice and the gentle guidance of the universe, Mr. Raaj learned to navigate the challenges that once seemed insurmountable.

He realized that spirituality was not just a beacon of hope in the darkness but a powerful force that could help him rise above his circumstances and emerge stronger and wiser than before.

Today, Mr. Raaj stands as a testament to the transformative power of spirituality and inner healing inspiring others to embark on their journey of self-discovery and inner growth to connect with a higher self.

His story serves as a reminder that even in the darkest of moments, there is always **a light that can lead us toward healing, transformation, and ultimately, a life filled with love and purpose.**

In Topic Conclusion:

These are just a few common areas where **"The art of believing"** can be practiced. Ultimately, it can be applied to any aspect of life where belief, trust, and confidence are necessary for personal growth, success, and fulfillment.

B. Benefits of practicing "The Art of Believing”.

There are several benefits of “The Art Of Believing”, including:

1. Increased self-confidence & Self-esteem:

Practicing **"The Art of Believing"** helps individuals develop a positive and confident mindset, which can lead to increased self-belief and belief in self-abilities. Ultimately it enhances **self-confidence and self-esteem.**

For Instance, Individuals who practice **"The Art of Believing"** often find themselves on a path to increased self-confidence and self-esteem. By cultivating a positive and confident mindset, they begin to trust in their abilities and potential.

This newfound self-belief can have a transformative effect on their lives, empowering them to take on new challenges with **courage and determination.** As they continue to nurture this mindset, they will see a boost in their self-confidence and a deepening of their self-esteem. Embracing the power of belief in oneself is a powerful tool for personal growth and development.

2. Improved Resilience:

Believing in oneself and having a positive outlook on life can help individuals develop resilience and bounce back from setbacks or challenges more effectively. Building resilience is like strengthening a muscle - the more you exercise it, the stronger it becomes.

For instance, when facing a difficult situation, maintaining a growth mindset can be incredibly beneficial. Instead of viewing obstacles as insurmountable barriers, individuals with strong resilience see them as opportunities for growth and learning. This mindset shift allows them to approach challenges with determination and creativity, ultimately leading to greater success and personal development.

By cultivating a resilient attitude, individuals can navigate life's ups and downs with grace and perseverance, emerging stronger and more capable with each new experience.

3 Enhances Self-Motivation:

Believing in self-goals and dreams can provide individuals with the motivation and drive to work hard, persevere, and achieve their desired outcomes.

For instance, envisioning the successful completion of a project or the accomplishment of a personal goal can ignite a spark within individuals, propelling them forward with enthusiasm and determination.

This self-motivation acts as a powerful force that pushes individuals to overcome obstacles, stay focused on their objectives, and ultimately turn their aspirations into reality.

By harnessing this inner drive and maintaining a positive mindset, individuals can cultivate resilience and tenacity in the face of challenges, enabling them to navigate through difficulties with confidence and grace.

In essence, self-motivation serves as a guiding light that empowers individuals to pursue their passions, realize their potential, and create a fulfilling life journey filled with purpose and achievement.

4. Emotional Well-Being: Reduces Stress and Anxiety.

"The Art of Believing" promotes a positive mindset and helps individuals develop coping mechanisms for managing their stress and anxiety in their critical circumstances. This can lead to improved mental well-being and overall happiness.

For instance, consider the scenario of a student preparing for a major exam.

By practicing **"The art of believing,"** the student can shift their focus from **self-doubt to self-belief,** helping them approach the exam with confidence and a clear mind. This positive mindset can reduce exam-related stress and anxiety, allowing the student to perform better and achieve their desired results.

Additionally, by incorporating techniques such as positive affirmations and visualization, the student can cultivate a sense of calmness and control during high-pressure situations, ultimately contributing to their emotional well-being and success in academics.

5. Increases Creativity:

"The Art of Believing" in oneself can unlock creativity and inspiration, allowing individuals to think outside the box and come up with unique and innovative ideas.

For instance, consider a scenario where a young artist decided to believe in their talent and pursue their passion for painting.

By nurturing self-belief and pushing boundaries, the artist was able to create extraordinary pieces that captivated audiences worldwide.

This journey of self-discovery and creative expression showcases the power of believing in oneself to unlock endless possibilities and push the boundaries of imagination.

6. Improves Better Relationships:

"The Art of Believing" encourages individuals to have a positive outlook on others, leading to improved relationships and better social interactions.

For instance, consider a case where two colleagues, Sarah and John, had a misunderstanding due to miscommunication. Instead of holding grudges or jumping to conclusions, Sarah decided to practice the art of believing in John's good intentions.

She approached him calmly, expressing her concerns and giving him the benefit of the doubt. John, feeling understood and not judged, explained his side of the story. This open and trusting communication led to a resolution, strengthening their relationships and fostering a more harmonious work environment.

By embracing the concept of "The Art of Believing," Sarah and John were able to cultivate mutual respect, empathy, and understanding.

They learned to see beyond initial assumptions and to approach situations with a positive mindset, ultimately creating a foundation for healthier and more fulfilling relationships in both their personal and professional lives.

7. Personal Growth and Development:

"The Art of Believing" fosters personal growth by encouraging individuals to challenge their old limiting beliefs and develop new skills and perspectives.

For instance, consider a case where an individual is hesitant to try new experiences due to a fear of failure. By practicing “The Art of Believing” in oneself, this person can gradually shift their mindset from one of doubt to one of possibility.

They may start by setting small, achievable goals and celebrating their successes along the way. With time and persistence, they can develop the confidence to step out of their comfort zone and embrace new opportunities for growth and development.

In essence, The Art of Believing is a powerful tool for personal growth and development. It empowers individuals to break free from self-imposed limitations and strive for their full potential.

By cultivating a mindset of positivity and self-belief, one can navigate life's challenges with resilience and optimism, ultimately leading to a more fulfilling and enriching existence.

8. Improved Decision-Making:

Believing in oneself can lead to increased self-trust and confidence in decision-making, allowing individuals to make choices aligned with their values and goals.

For instance, when an individual is faced with a difficult decision at work. By having self-belief and confidence, this person can trust their judgment and make the right choice that reflects their integrity and long-term objectives.

This can result in a more fulfilling and successful outcome, as they dare to stand by their decisions and take ownership of the results. Improved decision-making is not only about making the right choice but also about having the self-assurance to navigate through challenges with resilience and determination.

By fostering self-belief, individuals can empower themselves to make the right choices that positively impact their lives and lead to personal growth and development.

9. Enhanced Problem-Solving Skills:

"The art of believing" helps individuals develop a solutions-oriented mindset, enabling them to approach problems with a positive and proactive attitude.

For instance, consider the case of a college student who is struggling to pass an important exam. By embracing the concept of "The art of believing," the student can shift their focus from feeling overwhelmed to actively seeking out resources and strategies to improve their study habits.

This shift in mindset can lead to enhanced problem-solving skills as the student becomes more adept at identifying potential solutions and taking the necessary steps to overcome challenges. With perseverance and a positive outlook, the student can not only pass the exam but also develop a valuable skill set that will serve them well in their future endeavors.

10. Overall well-being:

Cultivating **"The art of Believing"** can contribute to a sense of fulfillment, purpose, and overall well-being, as individuals develop a positive mindset and live in alignment with their beliefs and values.

For instance, consider the case of a pregnant mother who has embraced "The art of Believing." Throughout her pregnancy, she holds onto the belief that she is capable, strong, and resilient.

This positive mindset not only helps her navigate the physical challenges of pregnancy but also provides her with a sense of purpose and connection to her growing baby.

By aligning her thoughts and actions with her belief in her strength and resilience, she can cultivate a deep sense of well-being and contentment as she prepares to welcome her child into the world.

This example illustrates how embracing **"The Art of Believing"** can have a profound impact on one's overall well-being and outlook on life.

C. Common Challenges to Practicing "The Art of Believing"

There can be several challenges to practicing **"The Art of Believing"**, including a Limited Belief System, Negative self-talk, Fear of failure, External influences, Lack of patience and persistence, Difficulty in visualization, Lack of clarity and focus, and Resistance to change.

Let's unravel the common challenges to mastering "The Art of Believing" and learn how to overcome them.

1. Limited Belief System:

Many people have old limiting beliefs established subconsciously in their minds, often due to past negative experiences or societal conditioning. Overcoming these old limiting beliefs can be a challenge as it requires questioning deeply held assumptions and beliefs.

For instance, a young woman named Sonika Thomas always believed she wasn't smart enough to pursue her dream of becoming a lawyer.

This belief stemmed from a teacher in high school who once told her she wouldn't succeed in a challenging course. As Sonika grew older, she realized that she had internalized this limiting belief and it was holding her back from achieving her goals.

One day, Sonika decided to challenge this belief by seeking out mentorship from successful lawyers and taking online courses to improve her skills.

With dedication and perseverance, she slowly started to dismantle the negative mindset that had been ingrained in her for years. As she gained more knowledge and confidence in her abilities, Sonika began to see herself in a new light - as a capable and intelligent individual capable of achieving her dreams.

It wasn't an easy journey, but Sonika's willingness to confront her old limiting beliefs and push past her comfort zone led her to a place of empowerment and self-belief. She eventually went on to pursue her dream of becoming a lawyer, proving to herself and others that she was more than capable of achieving success. It just goes to show that with determination and the willingness to challenge old beliefs, anyone can break free from self-imposed limitations and reach their full potential.

By challenging these limited beliefs and choosing to share your successes and joys with others, you not only empower yourself but also create a more uplifting environment for everyone.

Remember, true connections are built on authenticity and vulnerability, so don't be afraid to show your true self to the world.

Another example is a boy who was repeatedly told by his teachers that he wasn't good at math.

This feedback became ingrained in his mind, leading him to believe that he was simply not a **"math person."** As he grew older, this belief continued to hold him back, causing him to avoid math-related opportunities and challenges.

However, one day, he met a mentor who encouraged him to challenge this belief. With patience and support, the mentor guided the boy through difficult math problems, showing him that with practice and dedication, he could indeed excel in math. Slowly but surely, the boy's confidence grew, and he started to see himself in a new light.

Through perseverance and a shift in mindset, the boy not only overcame his old limiting belief about math but also discovered a passion for the subject. By challenging his assumptions and beliefs, he unlocked his full potential and proved to himself that he was capable of achieving great things.

These stories serve as a reminder that by confronting our old limiting beliefs head-on, we can pave the way for personal growth and success. It's never too late to rewrite the narrative we tell ourselves and break free from the constraints of our past experiences. With determination and a willingness to challenge the status quo, we can create a brighter future filled with endless possibilities.

2. Negative self-talk:

Negative self-talk can undermine one's belief in oneself and their ability to achieve their goals. Changing negative self-talk into positive affirmations requires consistent effort and self-awareness.

For instance, an unhealthy person who constantly tells themselves, "I'll never be able to lose weight, I always fail at diets."This negative self-talk can create a self-fulfilling prophecy, making it harder for the person to stick to a healthy lifestyle.

To combat this, the individual could reframe their thoughts into positive affirmations such as, "I am capable of making healthy choices each day and I am getting stronger and healthier with every positive decision I make." By consciously shifting their mindset in this way, they can build self-confidence and motivation to work towards their health goals effectively.

Another example is a lady who constantly doubts her abilities and criticizes herself for every mistake she makes. This negative self-talk can create a barrier to her success and prevent her from reaching her full potential. However, by recognizing this pattern and actively working to replace those critical thoughts with positive affirmations, she can start to build a healthier mindset.

Instead of saying, "I always mess things up," she can reframe it as "I am capable of learning from my mistakes and growing stronger." By practicing this shift in perspective regularly, she can gradually boost her self-confidence and cultivate a more positive self-image.

Remember, the power of positive self-talk can truly transform one's mindset and lead to a more fulfilling and successful life.

Exploring The Power of Words: How Our Words Shape Our Reality?

Words are powerful. **They have the ability to inspire, to heal, to connect, and to shape our reality.** We often underestimate the impact of our words, but the truth is that they hold immense power. From the simple phrases we use in our everyday conversations to the speeches that move nations, words have the power to influence **our thoughts, emotions, and actions.**

The famous quote by Ralph Waldo Emerson, "Words are alive; cut them and they bleed," captures the essence of the power of words. They have a life of their own, and when used wisely, they can create a positive impact on our lives and those around us.

Conversely, careless or hurtful words can leave lasting scars and create negative effects.

For Instance, It's no surprise that throughout history, leaders and activists have used words to bring about change and shape the course of history. **Mahatma Gandhi's** famous words "Be the change you want to see in the world" inspired millions to stand up against injustice and fight for their rights. Similarly, **Martin Luther King Jr.'s** powerful "I Have a Dream" speech ignited a movement for racial equality.

But it's not just famous leaders who have harnessed the power of words. In our daily lives, the way we communicate with others can greatly impact our relationships and interactions. The words we choose can either build someone up or tear them down. A simple "thank you" or "I appreciate you" can make someone's day and strengthen our connections with others.

In contrast, negative or hurtful words can cause **irreparable damage.** We've all experienced moments when someone's harsh words have left us feeling hurt or small. This is because our brains are wired to respond to language. Studies have shown that when we hear negative words, our brain releases stress hormones like cortisol, which can have a detrimental effect on both our mental and physical health.

Conversely, positive words have been found to release oxytocin, a hormone that promotes feelings of trust and connection. This is why hearing words of encouragement or praise can make us feel happy and motivated.

Furthermore, our language not only affects those around us but also shapes our reality. The way we speak to ourselves is also known as self-talk, Self-talk refers to the thoughts and messages we tell ourselves, consciously or unconsciously, throughout the day. It can be positive or negative, and it has a significant impact on how we perceive ourselves and the world around us.

Studies have shown that our self-talk can greatly affect our mood, behavior, and overall well-being. Positive self-talk involves using kind, encouraging, and optimistic words when talking to ourselves. It involves being aware of our inner dialogue and intentionally choosing to use supportive and empowering language. Conversely, negative self-talk is characterized by critical and harsh words that often lead to feelings of self-doubt, anxiety, and low self-esteem.

Thus, self-talk has a profound impact on our thoughts, emotions, and actions. Negative self-talk can lead to feelings of self-doubt and insecurity, while positive self-talk can boost our confidence and help us overcome challenges.

It's essential to be mindful of the words we use, both in our interactions with others and in our internal dialogue. By consciously choosing our words, we can create a more positive and empowering reality for ourselves and those around us.

But How Exactly do words hold so much power?

It's because words are not just empty sounds or letters. They carry meaning and energy, and when spoken or written with intention, they can evoke strong emotions and spark change. This is evident in the art of storytelling, where skilled writers can transport us to different worlds with their words.

Similarly, This is evident in motherhood when kids get hurt and the simple act of saying "I love you" can instantly soothe their pain. Words can uplift spirits, inspire individuals, and provide comfort during times of need.

Words also have the power to shape our beliefs and perceptions. We often use language to describe the world around us, but what we don't realize is that the words we use also influence how we see things.

For instance, if we constantly use negative words to describe a situation, we may start to see it as entirely negative. Conversely, using positive language can help us find the silver lining in a challenging situation.

In addition to shaping our reality, words also have the power to heal. This is why therapy and counseling often involve talking through our problems and finding ways to reframe them with more positive language. The simple act of verbalizing our thoughts and feelings can be cathartic and help us gain clarity and perspective.

It's crucial to use our words wisely and consciously. But with great power comes great responsibility. This means being mindful of our words' impact on others and choosing them carefully. It also means taking responsibility for the messages we put out into the world and ensuring that they promote positivity and inclusivity.

Remember, the power of words cannot be underestimated. They have the ability to shape our reality, influence our thoughts and emotions, and bring about positive change.

As individuals, we must use our words responsibly and intentionally to create a kinder, more empathetic world. You must be careful about the words you use, or the words you allow to be used in your house."

Thus Negative talk or Self-talk has a profound impact on our lives. It's important to recognize when negative self-talk arises and actively work towards changing those thoughts into positive affirmations.

By consciously challenging and reframing negative beliefs, we can empower ourselves and cultivate a more optimistic mindset.

Through consistent effort and self-awareness, we can shift the narrative we tell ourselves and ultimately have a positive impact on our lives.

Remember, you have the power to shape your thoughts and beliefs and ultimately the used words in a way that supports your goals and overall well-being.

3. Fear of Failure:

The fear of failure can hinder one's ability to fully commit to their beliefs and take necessary risks. Overcoming the fear of failure requires developing resilience and embracing failure as a learning opportunity.

For instance, In the case of the homemaker looking to start her career after a long hiatus, it is normal to feel apprehensive about the unknown and the potential for setbacks. Yet, by acknowledging this fear and understanding that it is a natural part of growth, she can begin to shift her mindset.

By reframing failure as an opportunity for growth and learning, she can build resilience and courage to take the necessary risks to pursue her aspirations. Each setback can provide valuable lessons and insights that will ultimately propel her forward on her journey toward a fulfilling career.

Embracing failure as a teacher rather than a foe can empower her to step out of her comfort zone, try new things, and ultimately achieve her goals with confidence and resilience.

Take another example, In the case of the engineer, it is crucial to understand that failure is a natural part of the design process. Engineers often face challenges and setbacks as they work towards creating innovative solutions.

Embracing failure allows engineers to iterate, improve, and ultimately achieve success in their projects. By viewing failure as a stepping stone to progress, engineers can approach their work with courage, creativity, and a growth mindset.

Remember, every failure brings valuable lessons that can lead to even greater achievements in the future.

4. External influences:

External influences such as criticism, societal expectations, and judgments from others can shake one's belief in themselves and their desires. It is important to stay grounded in one's own beliefs and not let external influences dictate personal beliefs.

For instance, a newly married girl may face pressure from various sources about how she should act, look, or make decisions. In these moments, it is crucial for her to remember her own values and aspirations, and to stay true to herself amidst the noise of external opinions.

By staying true to who she is and what she believes in, she can navigate through external influences with strength and authenticity. Remember, staying true to oneself is a powerful form of self-respect and empowerment.

Another example, imagine a tree standing tall during a storm. The winds may blow fiercely, trying to bend its branches and sway its trunk, but the tree remains rooted in the strength of its own core.

Similarly, we must stand firm in our values and aspirations, not allowing external forces to uproot us from our true path. Just as the tree finds stability in its roots, we can find resilience in our inner beliefs, weathering any external challenges that come our way.

By staying true to ourselves, we can navigate through the storms of life with grace and strength.

5. Lack of Patience and Persistence:

The Art of Believing is a long-term practice that requires patience and persistence. It is common for people to give up on their beliefs and desires when they don't see immediate results. Staying committed and consistent can be challenging but is crucial for success.

Lack of patience and persistence can be obstacles on the path to mastering The Art of Believing. This long-term practice demands dedication and a willingness to persevere through challenges. It's natural to feel discouraged when results aren't immediately apparent, but it's important not to abandon your beliefs and desires. By staying committed and consistent in your efforts, you are paving the way for success.

Just like a gardener patiently tends to their plants, nurturing them with care and dedication, your beliefs too require time and attention to flourish. **Remember,** the journey of belief is a marathon, not a sprint, so stay focused and trust in the process.

For instance, **a chronically ill person** does not believe in self-healing and gives up after a few weeks of trying alternative therapies. However, if they had practiced patience and persistence, they might have seen improvement over time.

The journey towards self-healing is not an easy one, but with dedication and a positive mindset, remarkable progress can be achieved. By cultivating patience and persistence, one can unlock the true power of belief and manifest incredible transformations in their life.

Another example is a school teacher who believed in the potential of every student despite their initial struggles. She patiently worked with each student, providing support and encouragement even when progress seemed slow. Her persistence paid off as she witnessed the transformation in her students over time.

By staying committed to her belief in their abilities, she helped them unlock their full potential and achieve success beyond what they thought possible.

Remember, You may encounter many defeats, but you must not be defeated. In fact, it may be necessary to encounter the defeats, so you can know who you are, what you can rise from, and how you can still come out of it.

6. Difficulty in visualization:

Visualization is a key component of The Art of Believing, where one mentally imagines and feels the desired outcome.

Not everyone finds it easy to visualize and imagine, making it a challenge to fully practice this aspect of belief.

For instance, some individuals struggle with forming vivid mental images, while others find it hard to sustain their focus during visualization exercises.

Overcoming this difficulty requires patience and practice. One approach is to start small, visualizing simple objects or scenarios before progressing to more complex visualizations.

Another helpful technique is to engage multiple senses during visualization, incorporating sounds, smells, and textures to make the mental image more vivid and tangible.

It's important to remember that visualization is a skill that can be developed over time with dedication and perseverance. By staying consistent and gradually expanding the scope of your visualizations, you can enhance your ability to manifest your beliefs through the power of imagination.

7. Lack of clarity and focus:

Without a clear vision and focus, it becomes difficult to believe in and manifest desired outcomes. Setting clear goals and maintaining focus can be challenging in a world filled with distractions and shifting priorities.

It is important to remember that clarity and focus are like a compass that guides us through the noise and helps us stay on course.

When we cultivate a clear vision and maintain focus, we are better equipped to overcome obstacles and setbacks that may come our way. By staying true to our objectives and staying focused on what truly matters to us, we can make steady progress toward turning our dreams into reality.

For instance, consider a doctor who is treating a patient with a complex medical condition. Without a clear diagnosis and treatment plan, the doctor may struggle to provide the best possible care to the patient.

In the same way, in our personal and professional lives, lacking clarity and focus can lead to inefficiency and missed opportunities.

One effective way to combat this lack of clarity and focus is to regularly revisit our goals, reassess our priorities, and make adjustments as needed. By doing so, we can realign ourselves with our vision, stay motivated, and navigate through any obstacles that may come our way.

Another Example is when driving on a dark road, we may not see the destination at first, but gradually it becomes visible. Similarly, in life, a lack of clarity and focus can obscure our path forward. It's essential to illuminate our way by setting clear goals and maintaining focus.

Remember, clarity and focus are not fixed attributes but skills that can be developed and honed over time. So, embrace the journey of self-discovery, stay committed to your dreams, and trust in your ability to steer your life toward the bright future you envision.

8. Resistance to Change:

Beliefs often require changes in thoughts, behaviors, and actions, which can be uncomfortable and challenging. Resistance to change can hinder progress in practicing The

Art of Believing. Change is a constant part of life, and it is something that we all have to deal with regularly.

For instance, From personal changes, such as moving to a new city or starting a new job, to larger societal changes like technological advancements or political shifts, change is inevitable. However, while change may be necessary for growth and progress, it is not always easy to accept.

Let's define resistance to change. it is the act of opposing or refusing to accept a change that is being proposed or implemented. This resistance can manifest in various forms such as denial, anger, fear, or even apathy.

It is a natural human response, as we are creatures of habit and tend to seek stability and predictability in our lives. Therefore, when faced with a potential disruption to our routine or way of life, we instinctively resist.

In fact, many people often resist change, preferring to stick to what is familiar and comfortable. Because they may fear the unknown or feel insecure about stepping out of their comfort zones. However, it's important to remember that growth and transformation often occur outside of our comfort zones.

Embracing change as an opportunity for personal development can lead to discoveries and a deeper understanding of oneself. By overcoming resistance to change, one can truly unlock the potential for growth and enhance the practice of The Art of Believing.

For instance, **consider an old lady in a family, who has always held onto traditional beliefs and values passed down through generations.**

She finds it difficult to accept new ways of thinking and doing things, as it goes against everything she has known and believed in for so long.

However, to truly embrace **The Art of Believing,** she must be open to exploring new perspectives and possibilities, even if it means stepping outside of her comfort zone. By gradually opening her mind to change and being willing to adapt, she can discover the beauty and richness that come with evolving beliefs and embracing new experiences.

Remember, change is not always easy, but it is often necessary for personal growth and development. It is very much needed for social adjustment.

In Topic Conclusion:

Overcoming these challenges requires self-reflection, self-discipline, and consistent practice. It is important to cultivate a positive mindset, surround oneself with supportive individuals, and seek inspiration and guidance from mentors or resources to stay on track.

By engaging in these practices, individuals can develop the resilience and determination needed to navigate through difficulties and achieve their goals.

Remember, progress may not always be linear, but every step forward, no matter how small, is a significant achievement in the journey toward personal growth and success.

Keep in mind that dedication and hard work never go unrewarded. You are sowing the seeds for success when you put in the effort and dedication toward your goals and aspirations.

Dedication and Hard work are like an investment in yourself, with the returns being the achievements and fulfillment you experience along the way. So keep pushing forward, stay focused on your dreams, and trust that your hard work will indeed pay off in the end.

"Life has so many colors and we should enjoy it."

Life is indeed a vibrant tapestry of experiences waiting to be embraced. Each day brings new opportunities to explore, learn, and grow.

Just like a beautiful painting with its myriad of colors, life offers us a palette of moments, both big and small, that paint the canvas of our existence.

It is up to us to appreciate the richness and diversity that each color brings, adding depth and beauty to our journey.

IV. How to Cultivate "The Art of Believing" In Everyday Life?

Practicing **The Art of Believing** involves cultivating a positive mindset, embracing optimism, and having faith in the higher self, inner self, the universe, and others around us.

Cultivating "The Art of Believing" In Everyday Life involves several key practices: here are some

1. Identify limiting beliefs:

Identifying and challenging limiting beliefs is essential for fostering **a mindset of belief and possibility.** By recognizing and addressing these beliefs, individuals can open themselves up to new opportunities and growth potential. It's a crucial step in developing a positive and empowering mindset.

Start by **recognizing any negative or limiting beliefs** that may be holding you back. These could be **self-doubts, fears, or worries**.

Certainly! A few examples are of limiting beliefs:

"I'm not good enough."

"I'll never be successful."

"Change is always bad."

"I can't do it because I'm too old/young."

"I'll never find true love."

"Money is the root of all evil."

"I can't be healed"

"I can't trust anyone."

Exploring Belief Systems: As previously mentioned in earlier sections, Our thoughts influence our actions, which in turn shape our behavior, leading to the development of our attitude toward the world. This cultivated behavior forms the basis of our beliefs and belief systems. To foster a positive mindset, it is essential to examine our thoughts carefully.

Have you ever questioned the origin of the beliefs you've acquired over the course of your life's experiences? Much of what you believe regarding happiness, love, respect, anger, or stress is heavily influenced by your social upbringing.

It's essential to take a moment to **reflect on these beliefs, acknowledge the ones that resonate with you,** and **let go of any limiting beliefs**. Our belief system shapes how we interpret every situation we encounter.

Our way of life greatly depends on various aspects such as **our thoughts, feelings, attitudes, habits, personality, and ultimately our destiny.** It is crucial to choose the right beliefs as they shape our future.

Common misconceptions **like the necessity of anger, finding happiness only in achievements, accepting stress as normal, letting external factors control our emotions, and more can hinder our progress.**

Embracing the idea **that anger is essential,** we tend to express anger frequently. Though we aimed for peace, it was fleeting. **Instead, Try out a new perspective,** Anger is harmful, and love is the key to productivity. By embracing this, love and joy will become second nature.

Let's swap out limiting beliefs for empowering ones. Remember, we assess each belief and embrace what serves us well. All our beliefs contribute to our **well-being, contentment,** and **alignment with our surroundings.**

Pause for a moment and reflect on the numerous beliefs you have embraced and carried since childhood. Have you taken the time to assess the beliefs concerning **yourself, others,** or **the world before internalizing them?** Or have you simply absorbed the beliefs imposed on you by your family, education, society, or past encounters? Our beliefs represent the ultimate truths in our eyes.

A belief system is like a scan disk, which stores all the pieces of information that influence our thoughts, words, and actions. Even one incorrect belief can have significant negative effects. It is essential to deliberately examine and replace limiting and inaccurate beliefs that hinder us from leading a fulfilling life. Take a moment to reflect and address beliefs that impede your personal development, happiness, and achievements.

How to recognize negative thoughts and beliefs?

Recognizing negative thoughts and beliefs is an important step toward managing and overcoming them. Negative thoughts and beliefs can manifest in various ways, such as **self-criticism, doubt, or catastrophic thinking.**

Let's understand catastrophic thinking.

Catastrophic thinking is a cognitive distortion where an individual excessively focuses on **the worst-case scenarios of a situation,** leading to heightened anxiety and fear. This type of thinking can be **irrational and unrealistic** and can prevent the individual from seeing the situation in a more balanced and positive light. It can also lead to feelings of helplessness and despair.

The development of a **"catastrophic thinking"** personality doesn't happen overnight. It begins with making **negative assumptions about oneself or others critically.** This escalates into increased concern and worry, leading to overthinking, and triggering fear.

Fear, in turn, fuels catastrophic thinking, resulting in unnecessary or Unproductive thoughts, negative internal dialogue or negative words for others, and negative intense actions or reactions. This cycle continues endlessly. Ultimately, individuals with a catastrophic thinking personality end up feeling helpless and despondent.

For instance, a man experiences job insecurity and catastrophizes about it.

Believing that he will get fired soon, which leads him to constantly worry and overthink every task at work. This excessive fear of losing his job creates a cycle of catastrophic thinking where he imagines worst-case scenarios like financial ruin and social embarrassment. As a result, he becomes more anxious and stressed, affecting his performance and relationships at work and home.

By recognizing and challenging this catastrophic thinking pattern, he can break free from the cycle and regain a sense of control and peace of mind.

Another example is a housewife who feels insecure about her marriage.

She tends to catastrophize situations involving her husband and her female coworkers.

This constant worry and fear lead her to overanalyze every interaction, imagining the worst outcomes possible. Every small issue becomes magnified in her mind, causing her to doubt her husband's faithfulness and her worth. This catastrophic thinking not only affects her mental well-being but also puts a strain on her relationship.

It's essential for individuals caught in this pattern to recognize these negative thought patterns and work on shifting their perspective to break free from the cycle of catastrophic thinking.

Therefore, Identifying negative thoughts and beliefs requires Self-awareness, Self-reflection, Introspection, and Mindfulness.

Here are a few steps to guide you through the process:

1.1. Pay attention to your emotions: Negative thoughts often trigger negative emotions like **sadness, anger, or anxiety**. Notice when you're feeling down or stressed and confused. By paying attention to your emotions, you can better understand your **mental state and address any negative feelings.** Take a moment to reflect on what may be **causing** your sadness, anger, or anxiety.

This **self-awareness and self-reflection** can help you develop strategies to cope with these emotions effectively. Remember, it's okay to feel these emotions, but it's important to acknowledge them and take steps to support your mental well-being.

For instance, a woman may find that her feelings of sadness are linked to work stress, while another woman may discover that her anger stems from unresolved family issues. By acknowledging these emotions and their underlying causes, women can begin to develop **personalized coping mechanisms**.

This might include engaging in self-care activities like exercise, meditation, or journaling, seeking support from loved ones or a therapist, and practicing positive affirmations to promote emotional well-being.

Remember, your emotions are valid, and taking steps to address them is a powerful act of self-care.

1.2. Pay attention to your conversation with others:

It's important to be mindful of the conversations we engage in with others. Negative dialogue can lead to harmful outcomes such as **self-doubt, misunderstandings, and unnecessary conflicts that only bring frustration and increase mental pressure.**

Negative conversations often trigger negative actions, notice when you're in a cycle of overthinking, feeling disgust, and feeling of hopelessness, where your minds endlessly circle the same topic.

If you find yourself caught in a cycle of overthinking, disgust, or hopelessness, it's crucial to take **a step back and evaluate** the impact of these conversations on your well-being. By being aware of the **tone and content of your interactions,** you can choose to steer them towards **more positive and constructive paths** that promote **understanding and harmony.**

For instance, a father may **unknowingly pass on his negative comments** or **self-talk to his children** through his conversations with them. His vocabulary might be that you are neglecting your studies completely. Your ability to focus on studying is lacking. You possess knowledge, yet you fail to apply it. You seem to be unproductive. This spoken vocabulary can create a cycle of **self-doubt and limiting beliefs** that may hinder the **child's growth and confidence.**

On the contrary, **positive** and **uplifting conversations** like you are making progress every day and getting better. We can see a new version of yourself emerging, your dedication to study is impressive, and your efforts are marvelous. Using positive vocabulary can **foster healthy relationships, build trust, and promote a supportive environment** where individuals can **thrive and succeed.**

By **paying attention to our conversations and choosing our words wisely,** we can contribute to a **more positive and harmonious atmosphere** in our interactions.

Remember, words have power, so let's use them to uplift and inspire those around us.

1.3. Listen to your inner dialogue: Be aware of the thoughts running through your mind. If you catch yourself having **self-critical** or **pessimistic thoughts,** they may be negative. Listen to your inner dialogue with **compassion** and **curiosity.**

Understand that the thoughts running through your mind are a **reflection of your inner world.** If you catch yourself having **self-critical or pessimistic thoughts,** gently challenge them with **kindness and understanding.**

Remember, you have the **power to shift your perspective and choose thoughts that uplift and empower you**. Embrace positivity and self-love as you navigate through your inner dialogue, and watch how it transforms your mindset and overall well-being.

For instance, when you are thinking of conflicting emotions, try to **explore the root cause of these feelings.** Are they stemming from **past experiences or fears** about the future? By delving deeper into **the source of your conflicting emotions,** you can **gain a better understanding of yourself and your triggers.**

Remember, it's okay to feel a range of emotions; what's important is how you acknowledge and process them. By nurturing a positive and compassionate relationship with yourself, you can **cultivate emotional resilience and inner peace.**

1.4. Pay attention to the criticism: Often people provide feedback **regarding our actions** and **behaviors.** Be mindful and actively listen to those comments. It could help shape our actions and behaviors positively.

Instead of **seeing criticism as a negative attack,** try to view it as an opportunity for growth and improvement. Embrace feedback as a chance to learn more about yourself and **how you can become a better version of yourself.**

For instance, a colleague in a workplace or any person in your relationship might provide feedback on your actions or behavior. Instead of feeling defensive, take their comments on board and use them to enhance your abilities and improve your qualities, try to change them with an advanced viewpoint.

Embracing constructive criticism is a valuable tool that can lead to personal and professional growth and increased confidence in your abilities. Always remember that feedback is a gift that can help you become the best possible version of yourself. By being open to feedback, you show maturity and a willingness to evolve.

1.5. Identify thinking patterns: Common and random thinking patterns that can lead to negative thoughts include catastrophizing (assuming the worst), black-and-white thinking (seeing situations in extremes), and over generalization (making broad negative conclusions from one event). By recognizing and understanding these thinking patterns, you can begin to challenge and reframe them.

Instead of **catastrophizing,** try to consider **alternative outcomes** and **possibilities.** Rather than seeing situations in black-and-white, look for other shades of life and nuance.

When faced with **overgeneralization,** remind yourself that one event doesn't define everything. By identifying and working to change these thinking patterns, you can cultivate a more balanced and positive mindset.

For Instance, a boy named James Anderson found himself constantly falling into the trap of catastrophizing situations. His mind would immediately jump to the worst-case scenario, leaving him feeling anxious and overwhelmed. However, with the help of a therapist, James began to identify this thinking pattern and learn how to challenge it.

He started to ask himself questions like **"Is this the only possible outcome?"** and **"What evidence do I have to support this catastrophic thinking?"** Through practice and patience, James gradually shifted his mindset and began to see situations in a **more balanced** and **realistic light.**

Over time, he found that he was able to approach **challenges with a greater sense of calm** and **confidence,** knowing that he had **the power to reframe his thoughts.**

1.6. Keep a journal: Write down your **thoughts and emotions daily**. This can help you **spot recurring negative thought patterns.** Keeping a journal is an excellent way to cultivate **self-awareness and understanding of your inner world.**

By jotting down your thoughts and emotions regularly, you create a space for **reflection** and **introspection.** Not only does this practice provide **an outlet for self-expression,** but it also allows you to track **recurring patterns in your mindset.** Over time, you may start to **notice certain triggers** or **themes** that are contributing to **negative thought patterns.**

By identifying these patterns, you can work towards addressing them and fostering a **more positive** and **balanced mental outlook.** So, grab a notebook or start a digital journal and embark on this journey **of self-discovery** and **growth.** Your future self will thank you for taking this proactive step towards emotional well-being.

Let's Spotlight, The story of Avantika embarks on a journey of self-discovery: Exploring her innermost thoughts and feelings.

As she pours her heart onto the pages of her journal, she begins to unravel the tangled web of emotions that have been clouding her judgment. Through the act of writing, she finds a sense of release, allowing her thoughts to flow freely without judgment or restraint.

In the quiet moments of meditation, **Avantika** delves deep within herself, seeking solace and guidance from her **inner wisdom.** It is in these moments of stillness that she begins to connect with her true **desires** and **aspirations.**

In therapy, **Avantika** finds a safe space to confront her **fears** and **uncertainties,** guided by a compassionate professional who helps her navigate the complexities of her emotions. Together, they explore the root causes of her **doubts** and **insecurities,** paving the way for **emotional healing** and **growth.**

Through these practices of **self-reflection and introspection, Avantika** gradually untangles the knots of confusion that have held her back, gaining a clearer understanding of her values and beliefs. With newfound clarity, she approaches her decision with **confidence and conviction,** knowing that she is guided by **the light of her authentic self.**

In Summary, Remember, Identifying negative thoughts and beliefs can be an ongoing process. Depending on person to person, how they cultivate and use it. Through **self-reflection** and **introspection,** one can change their perspective, which may hold them back. Engaging in this process will help you navigate and overcome negative and outdated limiting thoughts and beliefs.

2. Challenge Your Negative Thoughts and Beliefs.

Once you **identify** and **recognize** these old limiting thoughts and beliefs, you have **taken the first step towards freeing yourself from their constraints**.

Here are a few steps to guide you through the process:

2.1. Questioning Validity: Evaluate whether these beliefs **truly reflect reality** or **are merely assumptions.** Consider if they contribute to **your personal growth and well-being.**

It is important to **delve deeper into the beliefs** we hold and **question their validity.** By examining whether these beliefs align with reality or are based on assumptions, we can gain a better understanding of their impact on our **personal growth** and **well-being.**

Through **this process of critical evaluation,** we can cultivate a more nuanced perspective that allows us to navigate the complexities of our beliefs with greater clarity and insight. This practice of questioning validity **can lead to profound self-discovery and transformation** as we strive to align our beliefs with our truest selves.

For instance, a girl who always felt the need to please everyone around her realized that this belief was causing her undue stress and anxiety.

Through self-reflection and exploring different viewpoints, she discovered that setting healthy boundaries and prioritizing her well-being was essential for her mental health. This newfound understanding allowed her to embrace **self-care practices and lead a more balanced and fulfilling life.**

2.2. Evidence and Logic: Assess if these beliefs are **grounded in facts or are influenced by perceptions.** Often, negative beliefs lack a basis in reality and may stem from insecurities or past experiences that no longer apply.

It's important to **critically evaluate the evidence** of these beliefs by seeking out accurate information and considering different perspectives. Remember, our beliefs shape our reality, so it's essential to ensure they are rooted in truth and empathy.

For instance, a lady believes that if she eats a certain food, she will gain weight instantly. This belief may have originated from societal pressures or personal experiences.

However, **by examining the evidence and logic behind this belief,** she may discover that **weight gain is a complex process** influenced by various factors such as **overall diet, exercise, and metabolism.**

By seeking out accurate information and challenging misconceptions, she can develop a healthier relationship with food and her body, leading to a more balanced and positive mindset. It's crucial to remember that **our beliefs have the power to shape our perceptions and experiences,** so it's worthwhile to ensure they are **based on factual information and understanding.**

2.3. Empowerment to Change: Recognize that these beliefs are shaped by past experiences, societal norms, and personal perceptions, but you have **the power to challenge** and **transform them.** By acknowledging the influence of these factors, you can begin to take control of your narrative and shape your beliefs in a way that aligns with your true self.

One powerful way to initiate this change is through **self-reflection and introspection.** Embrace the opportunity to explore new perspectives and incorporate fresh ideas into your mindset. Remember, empowerment comes from within, and by embracing change, you can chart a path toward a more authentic and fulfilling existence.

2.4. Focus on Solutions: Shift your attention towards **solutions rather than fixating on problems** to foster a positive mindset. **For instance**, When you focus on solutions, you allow yourself to approach challenges with a more optimistic outlook.

Instead of **feeling overwhelmed by problems,** you can actively seek ways to address them. By shifting your mindset in this way, you empower yourself to take control of the situation and work towards finding positive resolutions.

"Focus on solutions rather than dwelling on problems."

Remember, every problem has a solution waiting to be discovered - it's just a matter of approaching it with the right mindset and determination.

2.5. Positive Reinforcement: Replace negative beliefs with positive ones by focusing on **your strengths and past achievements.** Seek support from friends, family, or a therapist for encouragement and positive feedback.

By acknowledging your strengths and past achievements, you can create a **strong foundation for building a more positive mindset.**

Remember, you are capable of overcoming any obstacles that come your way with a positive outlook.

3. Replace Negative Thoughts and Beliefs with Positive Ones.

Replacing negative thoughts and beliefs with positive ones is a key aspect of **cognitive restructuring,** a technique commonly used in **reprogramming the subconscious mind** or **cognitive-behavioral therapy** (CBT).

By replacing negative thoughts with positive ones, you are taking a proactive step towards improving your **mental well-being**. This shift in mindset is a powerful tool that can help reshape how you perceive yourself and the world around you. Through **cognitive restructuring,** you can **challenge** and **reframe those harmful thoughts** that may be holding you back.

One effective way to start this process is by practicing **self-awareness, self-reflection, introspection,** and **mindfulness.** By becoming more attuned to your thoughts and feelings, you can identify when negative patterns arise and consciously choose to replace them with **more positive and empowering alternatives.**

Maybe there's a formula you can apply in these situations.

"Pause, Check, and Change Formula."

Try this **Pause, Check, and Change Formula** with more **positive, balanced,** and **highly elevated ones.** By identifying these negative thoughts, you can begin to understand the **patterns** and **triggers** that contribute to them.

For instance, a boy who had a conflicting conversation with his dad may pause momentarily to acknowledge his feelings and thoughts.

Then, he can check in with himself to understand why he reacted the way he did. Was it due to past experiences, current stress, or miscommunication?

Finally, he can consciously try to change his perspective by focusing on the positive aspects of the situation. Perhaps he could **think about the love and care** his dad has shown him in the past, or consider the possibility of having a calm and constructive conversation in the future.

This **Pause, Check,** and **Change Formula** can help shift his mindset from negative to positive, allowing him to approach similar situations with a more optimistic and open mindset.

Initially, a **conscious effort** is required to adopt this approach, followed by a period of adjustment to the formula. Over time, your mind will effortlessly transition to autopilot mode to implement this technique.

Remember, it's okay to **acknowledge negative thoughts,** but it's essential not to dwell on them. Instead, focus on cultivating a mindset that is **kind, compassionate, and supportive** of your growth and overall well-being.

As you continue to practice replacing negative thoughts with positive ones, you will gradually notice a shift in **your overall outlook and emotional resilience.** This transformation takes **time and effort,** so be **patient and gentle** with yourself along the way that is aligned with your **true potential and inner strength.**

Therefore, recognizing and challenging these beliefs can be a powerful step toward personal growth and positive change. Through the process of self-discovery and personal development, people can cultivate positivity, a mindset of resilience, adaptability, and continuous learning.

As they strive to overcome their limiting beliefs, **they can embark on a journey of transformation that leads to a more fulfilling** and **purpose-driven life.** Embracing change and pushing past these barriers can pave the way for **endless growth and success.**

Remember that replacing negative thoughts with positive ones is an ongoing process that requires practice and patience. It may not happen overnight, but with persistence and effort, you can rewire your thought patterns and cultivate a more positive mindset.

However, you hold the power to challenge and change them.

For Instance: Take a **"Holy Bible's Reference": "As you Sow so you reap"!**

Galatians 6:7-8 NIV

6: 7 Do not be deceived: God cannot be mocked. A man reaps what he sows.

6:8 Whoever sows to please their flesh, from the flesh will reap destruction; whoever sows to please the Spirit, from the Spirit will reap eternal life.

This reference from the Holy Bible emphasizes the concept of reaping what you sow.

It serves as a powerful reminder **that every action we take, every word we speak, and every choice we make will have consequences,** whether **positive or negative.**

In essence, it encourages us to **be mindful of our deeds and the energy** we put out into the world, as they will eventually come back to us in one form or another form.

Just as **a farmer plants seeds and later harvests the crops,** our intentions and actions shape our destiny. By being **conscious of this principle,** and trying to **challenge our belief, we can strive to sow seeds of kindness, compassion, and positivity towards our goals and aspirations,** we can hope to reap a bountiful harvest of love and fulfillment in our lives.

Let's highlight a story: how a 47-year-old pregnant woman transformed her previous limiting belief that she couldn't carry a baby due to her health and advanced age.

She began by seeking support from healthcare professionals who provided her with guidance on maintaining a healthy lifestyle during pregnancy. She also engaged in prenatal yoga and meditation to foster a positive mindset and reduce stress. Through regular check-ups and monitoring, she was able to address any health concerns promptly.

Additionally, she surrounded herself with a strong support system of friends and family who encouraged and uplifted her throughout her journey. By focusing on her well-being and the well-being of her growing baby, she nurtured **a sense of empowerment and resilience.**

As her pregnancy progressed, she marveled at the strength and adaptability of her body, realizing the incredible capacity it had to nurture new life. Embracing this newfound belief in her body's ability to carry a baby, she radiated confidence and joy, eagerly anticipating the arrival of her little one.

Through **determination, positivity, and unwavering belief in herself, she shattered the limitations imposed by her previous beliefs,** proving that age and health should never stand in **the way of the miracle of life.**

Remember, **your thoughts have a powerful impact on your reality,** so by **cultivating a mindset of strength and possibility,** you can overcome **old limitations and embrace new possibilities.** Trust in your potential and the transformative power of your mind to manifest positive change in your life.

By actively challenging and reshaping these outdated beliefs, you pave the way for a profound shift in your mindset. Embrace **affirmations, visualization, and self-compassion to foster a more empowering internal dialogue.** Cultivate a sense of gratitude and self-love to nourish your inner world with positivity and resilience.

Remember, The journey towards **self-transformation begins with a single thought - choose wisely, and watch as your reality aligns with your newfound beliefs.**

4. Manage Your Emotions:

Managing emotions is crucial for fostering a belief in oneself and one's abilities. When emotions are well-regulated, individuals can approach challenges with confidence, maintain focus, and persevere through setbacks. This emotional resilience is essential for nurturing The Art of Believing in oneself and achieving personal and professional goals.

Effectively managing emotions **during challenging times is crucial for one's overall well-being.** We tend to overreact or exaggerate when the expected results are delayed, despite investing ample time and energy in achieving them. or we tend to be overwhelmed with emotional comments passed by someone, despite offering them adequate care and support.

It's important to remember that it's okay to feel frustrated or disappointed when things don't go as planned and expected. However, effectively managing these emotions can make a significant difference in how we navigate through tough situations.

Maintaining **a healthy emotional balance** by acknowledging negative emotions while not letting them overshadow positive ones. It's about **managing emotions constructively.**

One effective strategy is to practice **mindfulness and self-awareness.** Take a moment to identify **what you are feeling and why you are feeling that way.** This can help you **gain clarity and perspective on the situation,** allowing you to respond more **thoughtfully rather than impulsively**—practice **self-reflection as a " Pause, Check, and Change" Formula.**

External influences and interactions shape what comes to us and what we send out. Situations and individuals originate externally, so we have no control over what we receive from them. However, our reactions – **our thoughts, words, and actions** – are always **within our control.** It is common to attribute our emotions to others, but ultimately, how we respond is **our own choice**.

We often root the source of our happiness, anger, pain, or fear to someone else due to our tendency to place blame. Additionally, we may not always realize that our reactions stem from within us. **Let's make a conscious decision to respond with peace, calmness, and happiness.**

Remember, Our emotions are our creation, and no one else holds the power to control how we feel. We often attribute our emotions to others, but in reality, no emotion is self-evident, and no reaction is automatic. It's crucial to take ownership of **our thoughts, feelings, and actions.**

For instance, when our emotions are deeply involved, we act defensively and say He/ she upset me by his/her actions. His/her behavior made me angry, and it shouldn't be tolerated.

When we feel angry or upset at someone else's actions, it's easy to blame them for causing our emotions. However, it's important to remember that our emotions are our responsibility.

By **acknowledging and understanding our feelings,** we can better control our reactions and choose how to respond in a way that aligns with our values and beliefs. **Taking ownership of our emotions empowers us to act consciously** and **with intention,** leading to healthier relationships and greater emotional well-being.

Our happiness is not dictated by our circumstances but by **how we react to them.** It all starts with the thoughts our mind generates. Nurturing the mind with positive thoughts at the start of the day is akin to sowing healthy seeds in fertile soil. The external environment frequently mirrors our thoughts. Positive thoughts tend to bring about happy experiences and yield fruitful outcomes.

Be relaxed and program your mind for a perfect life. Set the foundation of emotional stability to build your responses. **Situations and people can be imperfect but your state of mind should remain perfect – calm, happy, and peaceful.**

Your thoughts, words, and actions should radiate positive vibrations, and energy, impacting people and situations positively. This will bring more peace and happiness, attracting more opportunities to grow and fruition.

Therefore practicing self-reflection of each thought and replacing it with positive and highly elevated thought is the right choice.

Additionally, engaging in activities that help you **relax and recharge** can help you manage emotions more effectively. Whether it's going for a **walk in nature, practicing deep breathing exercises, or spending time doing something you enjoy,** finding ways to **de-stress** can greatly benefit your **emotional well-being.**

Always remember, you are your greatest ally. Pay close attention to **your inner self and nurture yourself when necessary.** You have the power to recognize your emotions and make constructive transformations.

Therefore, it's okay to **seek support** from **friends, family, or a mental health professional** if you find it challenging to manage your emotions on your own.

Taking care of your emotional health is a crucial part of overall well-being, and by practicing **self-awareness and self-care,** you can navigate challenging times with **resilience and grace.**

5. Cultivate Positivity:

Certainly, **cultivating a positive mindset is a key aspect of nurturing- The Art of Believing.** When individuals maintain a positive outlook, they are more likely to see opportunities rather than obstacles, which bolsters their belief in their ability to overcome challenges and achieve success. Positive thinking fosters resilience, optimism, and a sense of possibility, all of which are essential for cultivating belief in oneself and one's potential.

Positivity referred to as a **positive mindset or attitude,** involves a mental and emotional **approach** to life that emphasizes **identifying the good, hopeful, and**

constructive elements or aspects in various situations and circumstances.

Exploring the constructive aspects: When exploring the topic of constructive aspects, it is essential to consider the **positive elements, strengths, and beneficial qualities** present in a particular situation, idea, or circumstance.

Emphasizing constructive aspects can help foster **growth, development, and progress**, leading to **innovative solutions and successful outcomes.** By focusing on **what works well and leveraging** these strengths, individuals can enhance their performance, build resilience, and achieve their goals and aspirations more effectively.

Recognizing and **nurturing constructive** aspects also promotes **a mindset of optimism, creativity,** and **collaboration, inspiring others to contribute positively** and **make meaningful contributions.**

Ultimately, embracing **constructive aspects** can lead to a **more fulfilling** and **impactful journey toward personal** and **collective success.**

Here are a few constructive aspects to practice: Shifting your mindset, focusing on the good things, surrounding yourself with positive people, being optimistic, practicing gratitude, encouraging positive self-talk, giving yourself credit, being resilient, being self-compassionate, being flexible, being empathetic and kind, being hopeful to people situation and any other circumstances.

Let's take a closer look at it more closely and approach its development with a positive mindset.

5.1. Shifting your mindset: towards a **more positive outlook** such as **compassion, gratitude, forgiveness, kindness, acceptance, flexibility, and adjustability.**

These can gradually be cultivated, especially when **we stop complaining about ourselves, people, situations, and any other circumstances** and **start to find solutions-oriented thinking.** Instead of dwelling on problems, a positive outlook seeks solutions and focuses on what can be done to improve the situations to overcome.

For instance, a working mother could shift her mindset by practicing self-compassion and understanding that it's okay not to be perfect. She could express **gratitude** for the support she receives**, forgive** herself for any shortcomings, and show **kindness** to herself and others.

By accepting that she may not be able to do everything perfectly all the time, she can embrace **flexibility** and **adjustability** in her approach **to work and family life.** This shift in mindset can help her navigate challenges with a **more positive and proactive attitude, leading to increased resilience and overall well-being.**

5.2. Focus on the good things in your life and practice welcoming those beautiful moments and events. Remember to appreciate the simple joys that come your way each day, whether it's a warm cup of tea in the morning, a friendly smile from a stranger, or a peaceful moment of solitude.

By shifting your **focus towards positivity,** you invite more of these wonderful experiences into your life. You can enjoy abundance. Embrace gratitude and let it guide you towards a more fulfilling and happy life.

We will delve deeper into the practice of gratitude in the upcoming chapter. Remember not to overlook that aspect, since gratitude is the key asset in our lives for attracting more fulfillment.

5.3. Surround yourself with positive people: who inspire and uplift you and give some **good suggestions. For instance,** in a moment of thought time, it can be helpful to reach out to a friend who is always **full of encouragement and positivity.** Engaging in a conversation with them can help shift your perspective and uplift your spirits.

Additionally, attending events or joining groups where you can meet **like-minded individuals who radiate positivity** can also be a great way to surround yourself with a **supportive community.**

Remember, positivity is contagious, so the more you immerse yourself in a positive environment, the more you are inspired to maintain a positive outlook in your own life. In the upcoming chapters, we will explore the support system in more detail.

5.4. Be Optimistic: A belief that **favorable outcomes are possible**, even in challenging situations. **Positivity sees setbacks as temporary and opportunities for growth.** It's important to cultivate a mindset of optimism in life's journey.

By choosing to focus on **the potential for good outcomes,** even in the face of difficulties, we open ourselves up to **a world of possibilities**. Viewing setbacks as **temporary roadblocks rather than insurmountable obstacles allows us to learn, adapt, and ultimately grow stronger.**

Remember, **optimism is not about denying reality but about acknowledging challenges while maintaining faith**

in our ability to overcome them. Embrace **positivity, stay hopeful, and watch how your outlook can shape your experiences for the better.**

5.5. Encourage Positive Self-Talk, and replace self-criticism with supportive and empowering thoughts: For instance, I can do it. I am good enough to do this task. This helps build self-confidence and resilience.

The way we speak to ourselves can greatly influence our thoughts, emotions, and actions. By cultivating **a positive and empowering self-dialogue**, we can uplift our spirits, boost our confidence, and navigate through life's challenges with resilience. When we catch ourselves engaging in negative self-talk, it's essential to reframe those thoughts into **more constructive and compassionate ones.**

Encouraging **mantras, affirmations, and reminders** of past successes can serve as anchors in moments of **self-doubt.** By fostering a kind and supportive inner voice, we can create a nurturing environment within ourselves that propels us towards our goals and dreams.

Remember, **the conversations we have with ourselves** are just as important as those we have with others. Let's strive to be our own **greatest cheerleaders,** offering ourselves the same **understanding, encouragement, and love** that we readily give to those around us.

In the symphony of self-talk, let our words be a melody of empowerment and self-belief, guiding us toward a brighter and more fulfilling existence.

5.6. Give Yourself Credit: It's important to acknowledge your accomplishments and give yourself credit for even the smallest achievements by patting yourself on the back.

Remember to celebrate your victories, no matter how small they may seem. **Taking a moment to acknowledge your accomplishments and give yourself credit can be a powerful motivator.**

So go ahead, give yourself that well-deserved pat on the back, and keep moving forward with confidence and pride. **You're doing great!**

5.7. Practice Gratitude: Appreciate and acknowledge the good things in your life, both big and small. **Gratitude fosters contentment and a sense of abundance.** We will delve deeper into the practice of gratitude, in upcoming chapters.

5.8. Be Resilient: The ability to **bounce back from adversity or setbacks** with a **can-do attitude.** Resilience is a **key component of a positive outlook.**

5.9. Be Self-compassionate: Treating yourself with kindness and understanding, especially in times of failure or difficulties. **Self-compassion** promotes a positive self-image. We will delve deeper into the practice of Self-compassionate, in upcoming chapters.

5.10. Be Flexible: Be open to change, and **adapt to new circumstances.** Positivity embraces opportunities for personal growth and development.

5.11. Be Empathetic and kind: Showing empathy toward others and practicing kindness. Positivity includes a desire to uplift and support those around you.

5.12. Be Hopeful: Believe in a better future, and have confidence that you can contribute to positive change.

In essence: Positivity doesn't mean ignoring challenges or denying the existence of negative aspects of life.

Instead, it involves facing challenges with a **constructive and positive mindset.** It's about **finding the silver lining, learning from experiences,** and **maintaining a sense of hope and optimism** even in difficult times. Positivity can have numerous benefits for mental and emotional well-being, relationships, and overall quality of life.

6. Visualize Successes:

Visualizing successes is one key aspect of embracing -The Art of Believing in oneself. When we imagine and focus on our achievements, we are more likely to manifest them in reality. By picturing ourselves reaching our goals, we program our minds to work towards them and overcome any obstacles in our way. Visualization helps us stay motivated and confident in our abilities, ultimately leading us to greater success. Embracing this practice can help us cultivate a positive mindset and believe in our own potential to achieve greatness.

Imagine yourself **achieving your goals and dreams.** Envision the feeling of accomplishment and pride that comes with succeeding in your endeavors. Picture yourself overcoming obstacles with ease and grace, and imagine the joy and fulfillment that success will bring to your life.

By visualizing your successes, you are setting the stage for them to become a reality. Embrace **the power of positive thinking** and let your imagination guide you toward a future filled with triumph and happiness.

"Remember, When you visualize, Then you materialize."

Visualization is a powerful tool that helps reinforce your belief in your abilities and strengthens your motivation. In the upcoming chapter, we will delve deeper into the topic of visualization and its techniques.

7. Set Realistic Goals:

Setting realistic goals is truly essential to embrace -The Art of Believing. Realistic goals allow us to focus on what is achievable and motivate us to keep pushing forward.

By setting realistic goals, we are more likely to stay committed and see progress, which in turn boosts our self-belief and confidence. It is important to set goals that are challenging yet attainable, as this will help us to reach our full potential and make our dreams a reality.

Ultimately, having realistic goals helps us to stay grounded and take consistent steps toward success.

Breaking down your goals into smaller, **achievable steps** will help you build confidence and reinforce your belief in your ability to succeed.

Track your progress, As you work towards your goals, make sure to track your progress along the way. By keeping track of your achievements, you can see how far you've come and stay inspired to keep moving forward.

8. Take action:

Taking action is mostly important when you practice -The Art of Believing. Believing in something is the first step, but without taking action to work towards your goals, dreams, or beliefs, they remain just thoughts in your mind.

When you take action, you give life and power to your beliefs. By putting in the effort to make things happen, you are actively working towards what you believe in and increasing the likelihood of success.

Action is what separates those who simply dream from those who achieve their dreams. It takes courage, determination, and hard work to turn your beliefs into reality. Without taking action, you will never know what you are truly capable of achieving. So, believe in yourself and your abilities, but also take action to make your beliefs come to fruition

Belief is not enough on its own; you must take action to turn your beliefs into reality. Start taking small steps towards your goals and build momentum over time. **consistency is key** when it comes to turning your beliefs into reality.

Stay committed to your goals and **keep pushing forward,** even when faced with challenges or setbacks. By staying focused and determined, you can **make steady progress** toward achieving what you truly desire.

Remember, **every small step you take brings you closer to your dreams. So, keep moving forward with faith and determination, and success will be within your reach.**

For instance, If you wanted to become an MBBS doctor. This is a noble aspiration that requires dedication, hard work, and perseverance.

To turn this belief into reality, you must take concrete steps towards achieving it. Start by researching the educational requirements and steps needed to pursue a career in medicine. Create a study plan, set specific goals, and commit to studying consistently to excel in your academic pursuits.

Furthermore, gaining practical experience through internships, volunteering, or shadowing professionals in the field can provide valuable insights and help you build a strong foundation for your future career. Additionally, networking with established professionals in the medical field can open up opportunities for mentorship and guidance.

Remember, becoming an MBBS doctor is a challenging yet rewarding journey that requires dedication and resilience. By taking consistent action, staying focused on your goals, and seeking support when needed, you can turn your dream of becoming an MBBS doctor into a reality. Believe in yourself, stay committed to your path, and never underestimate the power of hard work and perseverance in achieving your aspirations.

Therefore, Embrace the journey and trust in your ability to make things happen. Stay focused, stay determined, and keep moving forward.

Remember, "Your actions today will shape the reality you desire tomorrow."

9. Learn Time Management:

Learning time management is essential for embracing- The Art of Believing because it allows you to prioritize your beliefs, goals, and aspirations within the constraints of time.

Here are some steps to help you improve your time management skills:

9.1. Set clear goals: Define your beliefs and aspirations, and set specific, achievable goals that align with them. Having clarity about what you want to accomplish will help you prioritize your time effectively.

9.2. Prioritize tasks: Identify the most important tasks that align with your beliefs and goals, and prioritize them accordingly. Use techniques like the Eisenhower Matrix or ABC prioritization to distinguish between urgent and important tasks.

9.3. Plan your time: Create a daily or weekly schedule that allocates time for tasks related to your beliefs and goals. Use tools like calendars, planners, or digital apps to organize your schedule and stay on track.

9.4. Break tasks into manageable chunks: Break down large tasks into smaller, more manageable steps to avoid feeling overwhelmed and make progress more manageable.

9.5. Eliminate distractions: Minimize distractions such as social media, email, or multitasking, and create a focused work environment that supports your beliefs and goals.

9.6. Set boundaries: Learn to say no to activities or commitments that do not align with your beliefs or goals, and set boundaries to protect your time and energy.

9.7. Evaluate and adjust: Regularly review your **time management practices** to assess what is working well and what needs improvement. Adjust your approach as needed to optimize your productivity and alignment with your beliefs.

By mastering time management skills, you can prioritize your beliefs and goals, allocate your time effectively, and embrace the art of believing in yourself and your potential to achieve your aspirations.

"Yesterday's the past, tomorrow's the future, but today is a gift. That's why it's called the present." — Bil Keane

10. Embrace self-care: Emotionally, Physically, and Spiritually.

Absolutely! Embracing self-care in all dimensions—emotionally, physically, and spiritually—is essential for fostering- The Art of Believing in oneself and one's potential.

Here's how each aspect contributes to belief:

Embracing self-care involves nurturing your emotional, physical, and spiritual well-being to maintain balance and overall wellness.

10.1. Emotional self-care: Take time to acknowledge and process your feelings, whether through journaling, talking to a trusted friend or therapist, or practicing mindfulness and self-reflection. Engage in activities that bring you joy and relaxation, such as hobbies, spending time with loved ones, or enjoying nature.

10.2. Physical self-care: Prioritize activities that support your physical health, such as regular exercise, nutritious eating, adequate sleep, and staying hydrated. Listen to your body's signals and give yourself permission to rest and recharge when needed. Practice relaxation techniques like deep breathing, yoga, or massage to reduce stress and tension.

10.3. Spiritual self-care: Cultivate practices that nourish your spiritual well-being and connect you with a sense of purpose and meaning. This could include meditation, prayer, mindfulness, or engaging in activities that bring you a sense of transcendence or connection with something greater than yourself. Spend time in nature, reflect on your values and beliefs, and seek opportunities for growth and personal development.

By embracing self-care in all these dimensions, you can foster a holistic sense of well-being and resilience that supports you in navigating life's challenges and living authentically and fully.

11. Embrace Failure and Learn From It:

Embracing failure and learning from failure is essential to fostering -The Art of Believing. Failure is often seen as a negative aspect of life, something to be avoided at all costs.

However, failure is actually a necessary part of growth and success. It is through failure that we learn valuable lessons, gain a clearer understanding of our strengths and weaknesses, and develop resilience.

Embracing failure means accepting -**that setbacks and challenges are a natural part of life.** It means not being afraid to take risks or try new things, even if there is a chance of failure. By embracing failure, we open ourselves up to new opportunities for growth and learning.

Learning from failure is equally important. When we fail, it is important to reflect on what went wrong and how we can improve in the future. By analyzing our mistakes and learning from them, we can develop new strategies and approaches that can help us succeed in the future.

Ultimately, embracing failure and learning from it can help us foster the art of believing in ourselves and our abilities. By seeing failure as a stepping stone to success rather than a roadblock, we can approach challenges with a confident and positive mindset. This belief in ourselves can lead to greater accomplishments and fulfillment in all areas of our lives.

Failure is **a natural part of the learning process.** Understand that setbacks and mistakes are **opportunities for growth and improvement.** Use them as lessons to strengthen your belief in yourself and your ability to bounce back.

Embracing failure and learning from it is a key aspect of nurturing -The Art of Believing which further leads to growth and development. When we acknowledge that failure is a natural part of the journey toward success, we can shift our perspective from one of defeat to one of opportunity.

Every setback and mistake presents us with a chance to **learn valuable lessons, refine our skills, and enhance our resilience.** Instead of **letting failures discourage you**, see them as **stepping stones** on the path to achieving your goals. Reflect on what went wrong, identify areas for improvement, and use this knowledge to propel yourself forward. By facing failures head-on and extracting the wisdom they offer, you can strengthen **your self-belief and cultivate a mindset that is resilient and adaptable.**

Remember, it is through **overcoming challenges and learning** from our failures that **we ultimately grow and thrive.**

"So, embrace failure as a teacher, not a roadblock, and let it guide you toward greater success and fulfillment in your endeavors."

12. Surround Yourself with Support:

Surrounding with support and support systems is a great essence of cultivating -The Art of Believing. Having a strong support system can indeed foster belief in oneself and one's goals. It provides **encouragement, guidance, and reassurance,** which are essential elements in **nurturing confidence and perseverance.**

Seeking help from family, friends, and mentors can be a valuable resource when faced with challenges.

Friends, family, or mentors act as a guiding light in times of darkness. When faced with challenging situations, we often struggle to find a solution that may be right in front of us. Unfortunately, rather than finding a solution, we tend to dwell on the problematic issues, wasting our valuable energy and time. Wisely seeking assistance from family, friends, and mentors can be a valuable choice.

Friends, family, or mentors who believe in you, can provide **valuable encouragement and guidance.** Their **presence** brings **warmth to our hearts** and **clarity to our minds**. Their **support, pieces of advice, suggestions, and teachings,** can provide **different perspectives and solutions** that may not have been considered.

By reaching out to those you trust, you can navigate through difficulties with **greater ease and clarity.** Like beacons in the night, they illuminate the path ahead, offering **comfort and support, uplifting the spirit** when you need it most.

Their **wisdom and encouragement** help us navigate through life's challenges, **reminding** us that we are **never alone.** With their guidance, we find **strength, courage, and hope to overcome** any obstacle that comes our way.

So, let us cherish these **guiding lights** in our lives and **express our gratitude** for the unwavering **love and guidance** they provide.

Therefore, Surrounding yourself with support is essential on **your journey towards achieving your goals.** Their unwavering support can **bolster your confidence** and belief in your abilities, helping you **navigate challenges and stay motivated.**

Remember, it's okay to ask for help and lean on your support system during tough times. Together, you can work towards resolving the problems and moving forward positively.

"Make sure that You don't have to go it alone - let them lift you and your spirit when you are in vital condition".

13. Practice Positive Self-affirmation:

Practicing positive self-affirmation is a powerful tool for fostering -The Art of Believing in oneself. Positive self-affirmations involve **intentionally affirming positive beliefs about yourself, your abilities, and your potential.**

Positive self-affirmation is the practice of identifying and focusing on one's strengths, positive qualities, and achievements. It involves repeating positive statements or thoughts about oneself to boost **self-confidence, improve self-esteem, and cultivate a positive self-image and positive mindset.**

Positive self-affirmations are powerful tools to reclaim our thoughts. By practicing positive self-affirmations, individuals can challenge negative thoughts and replace them with encouraging and empowering statements.

Affirmations can be modified to address specific areas of one's life, such as career goals, relationships, or personal growth. By repeating these affirmations regularly, individuals can **rewire their beliefs and increase their confidence.**

"Remember, the way we speak to ourselves matters, so let's fill our minds with positivity and encouragement."

In the following chapter, we will delve deeper into affirmations and how they influence our lives. I'm confident that you'll stay focused on reading the upcoming chapters.

14. Patience and Persistence:

Patience and persistence are crucial elements for fostering -The Art of Believing in oneself and one's aspirations.

Building belief **takes time and effort**. Be patient with yourself and remain persistent even if things don't seem to be going the way you want. Trust in the process and keep moving forward.

Remember, **just like a seed needs time to grow into a beautiful flower, your beliefs also need time to take root and flourish.** Embrace each small step you take towards your goals, knowing that each one is bringing you closer to success.

Stay committed to your journey, trust in your abilities, and keep nurturing your beliefs with positivity and determination. **With patience and persistence, you will overcome any obstacles and reach the heights of your dreams.**

15. Cultivate Self-Awareness:

Cultivating self-awareness is indeed a crucial achievement for fostering -The Art of Believing in oneself and one's potential. Start by becoming **aware of your**

current beliefs and mindset. Reflect on how **these beliefs shape your thoughts, actions, and overall perspective on life.** Challenge your beliefs, Be open to **exploring new perspectives,** and consider how changing your beliefs could **lead to personal growth and development.**

As mentioned earlier, the chapters focus on increasing self-awareness by acknowledging strengths and weaknesses, recognizing unique talents and qualities, identifying limiting beliefs, understanding triggers and patterns, managing emotions, paying attention to words and actions, aligning with values and purpose, and more. By following these steps, individuals can empower themselves and unleash their full potential.

Practicing mindfulness, and engaging in activities that promote mindfulness, such as meditation or yoga. These practices can help you stay present in the moment, reduce stress, and improve your overall well-being. By cultivating mindfulness, you can better understand your thoughts and emotions, **leading to greater self-awareness.**

Remember, cultivating self-awareness is a powerful achievement that lays the foundation for fostering the art of believing in oneself. By understanding yourself more deeply, you can navigate challenges with confidence, overcome self-doubt, and pursue your goals and aspirations with clarity and conviction.

16. Set Positive Intentions:

Setting positive intentions is an essential element in fostering- The Art of Believing. Indeed, setting positive intentions is crucial in cultivating belief. By focusing on positive outcomes and actively directing our thoughts towards our goals, we can empower ourselves to believe in our ability to achieve them. Positive intentions serve as a guiding light, helping to keep us motivated and resilient in the face of challenges.

Clearly define the beliefs you want to cultivate and embody. Set positive intentions that align with **your values, goals, and aspirations.** This can be done through affirmations, visualizations, or journaling.

"Remember, When your intentions are clear, you take inspired actions that resonate with your words and beliefs. You manifest your thoughts and actions quickly into your life by aligning your thoughts and actions with your desires."

17. Practice Gratitude: Practicing gratitude is a key aspect of fostering- The Art of Believing.

When we cultivate a mindset of gratitude, we become more aware of the positive aspects of our lives, which in turn boosts our confidence and belief in ourselves. Gratitude helps us to appreciate our strengths, accomplishments, and the support we receive, reinforcing our belief in our ability to overcome obstacles and achieve our aspirations.

Cultivate **an attitude of gratitude** by regularly expressing appreciation for what you have and the experiences you encounter. This helps shift your focus from **scarcity or negativity towards abundance and positivity.**

It's important to note that **practicing gratitude doesn't mean ignoring negative experiences or emotions.** Rather, it means **acknowledging and accepting** them while also recognizing the good that exists alongside them. When we cultivate a **grateful mindset,** we're better equipped to handle difficult situations and find meaning in our struggles.

Studies have shown that gratitude can improve **our mental health, increase our resilience, and even enhance our physical well-being.**

So, whether we're feeling down or on top of the world, taking time to appreciate the blessings in our lives can have a transformative impact on our overall sense of happiness and fulfillment.

"Acknowledging the good that you already have in your life is the foundation for all Abundance."

18. Surrounding yourself with like-minded individuals:

Certainly, surrounding yourself with like-minded individuals who share your values and aspirations can be incredibly beneficial for fostering belief. Being around people who understand your goals, offer support, and encourage growth can create a positive environment where belief flourishes.

Additionally, these individuals can provide valuable insights, accountability, and inspiration, further reinforcing your belief in yourself and your abilities. Seek out and connect with people who share similar beliefs or a growth mindset. Surrounding yourself with like-minded individuals can be incredibly beneficial for your personal growth and development.

By seeking out and connecting with people who share similar beliefs or a growth mindset, you can **create a supportive**

network that encourages you to strive for your goals and aspirations.

These individuals can provide **valuable insights, advice, and motivation** to help **you navigate challenges and achieve success.** Engage in intellectual conversations, join communities or groups centered around personal development, and learn from others who embody the art of believing.

Remember, surrounding yourself with a positive and uplifting community can be a powerful tool in your journey toward self-improvement and fulfillment. It is a wise choice to foster -The Art of Believing.

19. Embrace Growth and Challenges:

Embracing growth and challenges is indeed the roadmap for future success, and it's closely intertwined with- The Art of Believing. By viewing challenges as opportunities for growth rather than obstacles, we develop **resilience, adaptability, and confidence** in our ability to overcome hurdles.

Believing in ourselves allows us to approach challenges with a positive mindset, knowing that we have the capacity to learn and evolve from them. This mindset not only propels us forward but also shapes our future trajectories and the traits we develop along the way.

See setbacks, failures, and challenges as opportunities for growth. Embrace the **process of learning and view mistakes as valuable lessons.** Use these experiences to reinforce your belief in your ability to learn and adapt.

Remember, every hurdle you overcome and every setback you face is an opportunity to reinforce your belief in **your ability to learn, adapt, and grow.**

Embrace challenges as **stepping stones on your journey to success,** and you'll continually **evolve into the best version of yourself.**

"Acknowledging that perfection is unattainable, everyone experiences mistakes at some point."

It is important to remember that **making mistakes is a natural part of being human.** Each mistake we make provides an opportunity for growth and learning. Instead of **being discouraged by our imperfections,** we can choose to embrace them as valuable lessons that **shape us into better versions of ourselves.**

By accepting **our mistakes with grace and understanding,** we can move forward with confidence and resilience.

"Remember, it's not about being perfect; it's about how we choose to learn and grow from our mistakes that truly matter."

20. Continuously Learn and Explore:

Expand your knowledge and understanding of different perspectives, philosophies, and belief systems. By continuously learning and exploring, you open yourself up to a world of endless possibilities and growth.

Embrace the opportunity to expand your knowledge by **delving into different perspectives, philosophies, and belief systems.** By doing so, you not only **broaden your**

understanding of the world but also foster empathy and respect for diverse ways of thinking.

Remember, the pursuit of knowledge is a journey without end, **so keep your curiosity alive and your mind open to new ideas and experiences.** Read books, listen to podcasts, attend workshops or seminars, and engage in activities that challenge your existing beliefs and broaden your worldview.

"Life is a Learning Journey,
Full of Exciting Chapters."

View every part of your life as **a new chapter for learning,** whether it involves a **person, situation, circumstances, or even a stranger.** Life is a learning journey, we come to earth to learn from every aspect of life and renovate ourselves with the knowledge gained.

Embrace each experience as an opportunity to **grow, evolve, and expand your understanding** of the world around you. **Every interaction, every challenge, every success, and even every failure** or **negative encounter with a person, place, or situation**, is a chance to learn more about yourself and the strength to sustain in the world.

Approach each chapter with **an open mind and a willingness to learn,** and you'll find that life becomes **a rich tapestry of experiences** that shape and mold you into the **best version of yourself.**

"Remember, the more you Learn,
the more you Grow."

21. Stay Away from Negativity:

Avoid individuals or environments that consistently trigger negativity and drain your energy. Avoiding negativity can be beneficial for maintaining mental well-being and fostering a positive outlook on life.

Surrounding yourself with positivity, whether it's through uplifting relationships, constructive activities, or empowering thoughts, can help cultivate a more optimistic mindset. Practice gratitude, and engage in activities that bring you joy and fulfillment.

"Remember, Focus on -What You Can Control"

22. Don't Let Others Influence You:

Influence from others can significantly impact **our thoughts, emotions, and behaviors.** It's important to surround yourself with supportive and positive individuals who uplift and encourage you.

However, it's also crucial to be mindful of the influence of negative or toxic people, as their attitudes and behaviors can potentially drag you down. Setting boundaries, maintaining assertiveness, and consciously choosing the company you keep can help mitigate the impact of negative influences and preserve your mental well-being.

Additionally, developing **self-awareness and a strong sense of identity** can empower you to resist negative peer pressure and stay true to your values and goals.

How to avoid other's influence on our lives?

Avoiding the influence of others entirely may not always be possible or desirable, as human beings are inherently social creatures and interaction with others is a fundamental aspect of life.

However, you can minimize the negative impact of others' influence by implementing the following strategies:

22. 1. Self-awareness: Develop a strong understanding of your own values, beliefs, and goals. This will help you stay grounded in your identity and make decisions that align with your authentic self.

22. 2. Set boundaries: Clearly define your boundaries and communicate them assertively to others. This includes setting limits on the type of behavior or influence you're willing to tolerate from others.

22. 3. Choose your company wisely: Surround yourself with people who support and uplift you, and minimize your exposure to individuals who drain your energy or have a negative influence on your mindset.

22. 4. Practice critical thinking: Evaluate the information and opinions presented by others critically, rather than automatically accepting them at face value. Consider the source, evidence, and potential biases behind their viewpoints.

22. 5. Assertiveness: Learn to assert your own opinions, preferences, and decisions confidently, even in the face of opposition or disagreement from others.

22. 6. Develop resilience: Build resilience to external influences by cultivating a strong sense of **self-confidence, self-esteem, and emotional intelligence**. This will help you maintain perspective and bounce back from any negative influence more effectively.

Remember that while it's important to minimize the negative influence of others, it's also valuable to remain open-minded and receptive to constructive feedback and differing perspectives that can contribute to personal growth and development.

23. Avoid Argument:

Certainly! Avoiding arguments is often a wise choice to maintain harmony and peace in conversations and relationships. Focus on understanding, empathy, and constructive dialogue instead.

Consequences of the argument.

Arguments can lead to various consequences, such as strained relationships, hurt feelings, misunderstandings, and even escalation into more serious conflicts. They can also hinder effective communication and problem-solving. It's important to handle disagreements with care and respect to minimize negative outcomes. Choose kindness and compassion in your interactions, and you'll pave the way for positive communication and stronger connections.

Remember, when faced with differing opinions, it's important to approach the situation with an open mind and a willingness to listen.

"With patience and respect, you can create a safe space for healthy discussions, that fosters mutual understanding and growth."

24. Cultivate the Positive Energy:

Cultivating positive energy involves fostering a mindset of optimism, gratitude, kindness, and mindfulness. Engage in activities that bring you joy, surround yourself with supportive people, practice self-care, and focus on the present moment. By nurturing positivity within yourself, you can spread it to others and create a more uplifting and harmonious environment.

"Remember, Cultivating the positive energy within you is like planting seeds of happiness and peace that will bloom and flourish in your life."

Embrace challenges as opportunities for growth, and always choose to see the good in every situation. Your positive energy will not only uplift those around you but also attract more positivity into your life.

Be Sure, your mindset is a powerful tool, so nurture it with love, compassion, and optimism. Cultivate the positive energy within you, and watch how it transforms your world into a brighter and more beautiful place.

25 . Spread the Positive Energy:

Absolutely! Spreading positive energy is a wonderful way to uplift others and create a ripple effect of happiness and positivity. **Here are some ways to spread positive energy:**

25. 1. Smile: Smile at people you encounter throughout your day. A genuine smile can brighten someone's mood and create a positive connection.

25. 2. Kind words: Offer compliments and words of encouragement to friends, family, colleagues, and even strangers. A few kind words can make a big difference in someone's day.

25. 3. Acts of kindness: Perform random acts of kindness, such as holding the door open for someone, helping a neighbor with their groceries, or paying for someone's coffee. Small gestures can have a big impact.

25. 4. Listen actively: Be present and attentive when someone is speaking to you. Show empathy and understanding, and offer support when needed.

25. 5. Share positivity: Share inspiring quotes, stories, or experiences on social media or with those around you. Spread messages of hope, love, and resilience.

25. 6. Be an example for others: Be a positive role model by embodying kindness, compassion, and optimism in your actions and interactions.

25. 7. Express gratitude: Express gratitude for the people and things you appreciate in your life. A heartfelt thank you can make someone feel valued and appreciated.

"Remember, By spreading positive energy, you not only brighten someone else's day but also contribute to creating a more uplifting and harmonious world."

26. Understand Others Emotions

Understanding others' emotions involves empathy, active listening, and being attentive to nonverbal cues. It's important to put yourself in their shoes, acknowledge their feelings, and respond with compassion and support.

Pay attention to their tone of voice, facial expressions, and body language to gain insight into how they're feeling.

Validate their emotions and offer empathy without judgment. This helps foster trust, connection, and healthier relationships.

Intentionally, people, they won't hurt us.

Indeed, most people do not intentionally set out to hurt others. It's essential to recognize that hurtful behavior often stems from a place of their own pain, insecurities, or lack of awareness rather than a deliberate desire to cause harm.

Remember, By understanding this, we can approach challenging situations with compassion and seek to address underlying issues rather than reacting defensively. This mindset promotes empathy, forgiveness, and healthier interactions with others.

"To truly understand others, we must first learn to see things from their perspective."

27. Try To Navigate the Problem.

Navigating problems involves approaching them with a solution-oriented mindset and seeking constructive ways to address challenges.

Here are steps to navigate problems effectively:

27. 1. Identify the problem: Clearly define the issue at hand, including any underlying factors or contributing elements.

27. 2. Gather information: Collect relevant information and perspectives to gain a comprehensive understanding of the problem.

27. 3. Generate possible solutions: Brainstorm potential solutions or approaches to address the problem, considering different perspectives and creative ideas.

27. 4. Evaluate options: Assess the pros and cons of each potential solution, considering feasibility, effectiveness, and potential consequences.

27. 5. Choose a course of action: Select the solution that seems most viable and appropriate based on your evaluation.

27. 6. Implement the solution: Take action to implement the chosen solution, carefully following through with the necessary steps.

27. 7. Monitor progress: Keep track of the results of your actions and make adjustments as needed to ensure progress toward resolving the problem.

27. 8. Seek feedback: Be open to feedback from others involved in or affected by the problem, and use it to refine your approach and improve outcomes.

"Remember, By navigating problems systematically and thoughtfully, you can address challenges effectively and work toward positive resolutions."

28. Help Others With Intentions, Words, Actions and Emotions:

Certainly! When helping others, it's important to consider various aspects to offer meaningful support.

Here's how you can help others with intentions, words, actions, and emotions:

28. 1. Intentions: Approach the situation with genuine care and empathy. Your intention should be to genuinely assist the person in need without expecting anything in return. Focus on their well-being and how you can make a positive difference in their life.

28. 2. Words: Choose your words carefully to offer encouragement, reassurance, and empathy. Be mindful of how you communicate, using language that is supportive, non-judgmental, and respectful. Offer kind and uplifting words that validate their feelings and experiences.

28. 3. Actions: Take practical steps to provide assistance or support. This could involve offering a helping hand, providing resources or information, or actively listening to their concerns. Be proactive in your actions and follow through on any commitments or promises you make.

28. 4. Emotions: Show empathy and understanding towards their emotions. Validate their feelings and let them know that it's okay to feel the way they do. Offer comfort and support by being present, offering a listening ear, and showing compassion.

Remember, By combining intentions, words, actions, and emotions in your efforts to help others, you can provide meaningful support and make a positive impact on their lives. Let us strive to always help others with sincerity and warmth, knowing that even the smallest gestures can make a big difference in someone's life.

"Helping others with pure intentions, kind words, thoughtful actions, and genuine emotions is a powerful way to positively impact the world."

29. Discover a Better Version of Yourself:

"Discovering a better version of yourself" is about engaging in self-reflection, exploring personal growth opportunities, and making positive changes to enhance various aspects of your life.

This journey involves gaining self-awareness, setting goals aligned with your values and aspirations, and actively pursuing self-improvement. It can encompass areas such as mental and emotional well-being, physical health, relationships, career development, and personal fulfillment.

Remember, Embracing this process allows you to unlock your full potential and live a more fulfilling and meaningful life.

"You have the potential to improve yourself every day. Don't underestimate the power of a positive mindset."

30. Avoid Procrastination:

Avoiding procrastination is an essential key step for fostering a belief in oneself and one's abilities. Procrastination often leads to **self-doubt and undermines confidence,** as it creates a cycle of delay and avoidance.

By overcoming procrastination and taking action towards goals and aspirations we demonstrate belief in our capacity to accomplish tasks and overcome challenges. This proactive approach reinforces a positive mindset and builds momentum, ultimately contributing to greater self-assurance and belief in our potential.

"Avoiding procrastination is crucial for maximizing productivity and achieving goals and aspirations."

It involves taking proactive steps to manage time effectively, prioritize tasks, and maintain focus on important objectives. Strategies for overcoming procrastination include breaking tasks into smaller, manageable steps, setting deadlines, eliminating distractions, and cultivating a positive mindset.

"Remember, By tackling tasks promptly and consistently, you can enhance efficiency, reduce stress, and make significant progress toward your objectives."

31. Maintain Records of Your Progress and Accomplishments:

Maintaining records of your progress and accomplishments is a valuable practice for several reasons. It allows you to track your growth over time, celebrate your achievements, and stay motivated.

Additionally, reviewing your progress can help you identify patterns, areas for improvement, and future goals. Keeping records provides a tangible reminder of how far you've come and reinforces belief in your ability to succeed.

Whether it's a journal, spreadsheet, or other tracking methods such as sticky notes, wall frames, achievement boards, photos, videos, or any other documentation methods, etc.

Remember, Documenting your journey can be a powerful tool for fostering **self-confidence and belief in your capabilities.** So capturing your journey is not just a way to track progress but a means to celebrate your growth and inspire others along the way.

"Capturing your progress and achievements is a wonderful milestone, like finding a gem along your journey.

Looking back each year can provide the strength and courage to accomplish more."

Reflect on your life periodically, and you will appreciate the journey you have traveled. You have overcome challenges and obstacles with your abilities and divine guidance.

As you reflect upon your life's journey, take a moment to closely examine:

" Who you were in the past and who you are in the present."

Consider the changes that have taken place in your life, the challenges you have faced, and the decisions you have made. By analyzing your past and your present, you can gain a deeper understanding of your personal growth and development.

32. Learn the Emotional Coping Mechanism:

Coping mechanisms are strategies individuals use to deal with stress, adversity, or difficult emotions. These mechanisms can be adaptive or maladaptive, depending on how effectively they help the individual manage their emotions and navigate challenging situations.

Some common coping mechanisms include seeking social support, engaging in relaxation techniques, problem-solving, positive reframing, engaging in hobbies or activities, physical exercise, setting boundaries, and seeking professional help when needed. It's important for individuals to identify healthy coping mechanisms that work best for them and to practice self-awareness to recognize when they might need additional support.

These mechanisms help individuals regulate their emotional responses and navigate difficult experiences more effectively. Examples of emotional coping mechanisms include -Mindfulness and Meditation, Expressive writing, Emotional expression, Self-compassion, Cognitive reframing, Engaging in creative activities, and Pursuing creative outlets such as art, music, or dance can provide a means of self-expression, Emotional release, and Physical relaxation techniques.

These coping mechanisms can vary in effectiveness depending on individual preferences and circumstances, so individuals need to explore and identify what works best for them.

Remember, Learning the emotional mechanism is an essential skill that can greatly improve your well-being and mental health.

"Your emotional well-being is a priority, and taking proactive steps to cultivate healthy coping mechanisms is a valuable investment in yourself."

33. Cultivate a Self-driven Power Within:

Cultivating self-driven power within is indeed a crucial aspect of embracing -The Art of Believing in oneself. When you possess self-driven power, you tap into your **inner motivation, determination, and resilience,** which are essential for achieving your goals and realizing your dreams.

"Enjoy the One-man Army Within You."

Here's how cultivating self-driven power contributes to the art of believing:

33. 1. Inner Motivation: Self-driven power comes from within, driven by your **intrinsic desires, passions, and values.** When you're motivated from within, you're less dependent on external factors for validation or approval, allowing you to stay focused and committed to your goals despite obstacles or setbacks.

33. 2. Sense of Empowerment: Cultivating self-driven power empowers you to take control of your life and pursue your aspirations with **confidence and conviction.** You believe in your ability to create positive change and shape your own destiny, rather than being at the mercy of external circumstances.

33. 3. Resilience and Persistence: Self-driven power strengthens your resilience and ability to persevere in the face of challenges or failures. You bounce back from setbacks with renewed determination, seeing them as opportunities for growth and learning rather than reasons to give up.

33. 4. Confidence and Self-Belief: As you cultivate self-driven power, you develop a deep sense of confidence and self-belief in your capabilities. You trust in your skills, talents, and potential to overcome obstacles and achieve success, fueling your belief in yourself and your ability to realize your goals.

33. 5. Ownership and Responsibility: Cultivating self-driven power involves taking ownership of your **actions, choices, and outcomes.** You recognize that you have the power to shape your life and take responsibility for making decisions aligned with your goals and values.

33. 6. Alignment with Purpose: When you're driven by self-power, you're more likely to align your actions with **your purpose and values.** You have a clear sense of direction and focus, knowing what truly matters to you and dedicating your efforts to pursuits that align with your authentic self.

Remember, By cultivating self-driven power within yourself, you strengthen your belief in your ability to create the life you desire and overcome any obstacles along the way. It's an essential ingredient in -The Art of Believing in yourself and realizing your full potential.

"Jodi tor daak shune keu na aashe, Tobe Ekla Cholo Re".

This is a line from a famous Bangla poem by **Rabindranath Tagore,** an Indian poet, writer, playwright, and composer. It means that one should not expect anyone to come to their aid when they call out for help. In such a situation, one should continue on their journey alone.

34. Cultivate a Self-disciplined Power Within Yourself:

Cultivating self-discipline is indeed essential for harnessing-The Art of Believing in oneself. Self-discipline provides the **structure, focus, and consistency** needed to pursue your goals with determination and resilience.

Here's how cultivating self-disciplined power contributes to the art of believing:

34. 1. Consistent Action: Self-discipline enables you to take **consistent action towards your goals, even when faced with distractions or challenges.** By maintaining a disciplined approach, you build momentum and make steady progress towards your aspirations, reinforcing your belief in your ability to achieve them.

34. 2. Overcoming Procrastination: Self-discipline helps you overcome **procrastination** and **resist the temptation to procrastinate** on tasks or goals that are important to you. By prioritizing your time and energy effectively, you demonstrate your commitment to your goals, strengthening your belief in your ability to follow through.

34. 3. Building Habits: Cultivating self-discipline involves establishing **positive habits that support your goals and well-being.** Whether it's setting a regular exercise routine, practicing mindfulness, or allocating time for skill development, cultivating discipline habits reinforces your belief in your ability to create positive change in your life.

34. 4. Resilience in Adversity: Self-discipline fosters resilience by helping you stay focused and composed during challenging times. When faced with setbacks or obstacles, your disciplined mindset enables you to persevere and find solutions, rather than succumbing to self-doubt or negativity.

34. 5. Personal Integrity: Self-discipline is a reflection of your personal integrity and commitment to your values. By honoring your commitments to yourself and others, you build trust and confidence in your ability to follow through on your intentions, strengthening your belief in your character and capabilities.

34. 6. Freedom and Empowerment: Contrary to common misconception, self-discipline does not restrict freedom; instead, it empowers you to act in alignment with your goals and values. By exercising self-control and making conscious choices, you gain a sense of autonomy and empowerment, reinforcing your belief in your capacity to shape your destiny.

Self-disciplined Power: With self-discipline, one can achieve great feats and unlock their inner power. Self-discipline is like a muscle that can be strengthened through practice and perseverance.

It allows individuals to stay focused on their goals, resist temptations, and overcome obstacles that may come their way. When one harnesses the power of self-discipline, one can cultivate a sense of control over their actions and decisions, leading to personal growth and success.

Remember, self-discipline is not about depriving oneself, but rather about making conscious choices that align with one's values and aspirations. Embrace self-discipline as a tool to unlock your full potential and create the life you desire.

34. 7. Self-Confidence: Cultivating self-discipline boosts your self-confidence as you witness your ability to set goals, stick to your plans, and achieve results. Each success further solidifies your belief in your competence and worthiness, fueling a positive cycle of self-belief and achievement.

Remember, cultivating self-discipline is essential for harnessing the art of believing in oneself. It provides the structure, focus, and resilience needed to pursue your goals with confidence and determination, ultimately empowering you to realize your full potential and create the life you desire.

"Self-discipline is like a precious jewel for someone. It shines brightly, casting a glow of empowerment and assurance in every step taken."

35. Cultivate the Belief in a Higher Self: Believing in your higher self involves having faith in your **inner wisdom, intuition, and potential for growth and fulfillment.** It's about trusting in your ability to overcome challenges, make positive choices, and live in alignment with your values and aspirations.

Cultivating a belief in your higher self can empower you to tap into your inner strength, resilience, and creativity, guiding you towards a more purposeful and fulfilling life.

"Cultivating the belief in a higher self is like confidently and effortlessly ascending an escalator toward your destination."

We will look at deeper aspects of higher-self in upcoming chapters. So keep reading and empower yourself.

36. Cultivate the Belief in the Universe: Believing in the universe involves having faith in the interconnectedness of all things and trusting in the natural flow of life. It's about recognizing that there is a higher order or energy that guides and supports us, even in times of uncertainty.

This belief can provide a sense of peace, purpose, and alignment with the greater forces at work in the universe. By cultivating trust in the universe, we can surrender control, embrace the present moment, and open ourselves to opportunities and synchronicities that align with our highest good.

"Cultivating a belief in the universe is like discovering a treasure that adds value to our life for the long term."

Embrace the mysteries of the cosmos and let the universe guide you towards a more fulfilling and enlightening path.

37. Cultivate The Belief in Others: Believing in others involves having faith in their capabilities, potential, and inherent worth. When you believe in others, you acknowledge their strengths, talents, and capacity for growth.

This belief can inspire and motivate them to reach their goals, overcome obstacles, and realize their full potential. By fostering a culture of belief and support, we can create environments where individuals feel empowered to thrive and contribute positively to their communities and the world.

"Believing in others is like a ray of light to a fading flame."

This statement emphasizes the importance of cultivating belief in others and the transformative effect it can have. It has the power to reignite the spark of hope and inspiration within them, casting away the shadows of doubt and uncertainty.

"Believing in others is like showing a light in their darkness."

When we believe in others, we offer them not just our confidence, but also our unwavering support and encouragement. Like a bolt of lightning piercing through the darkness, our belief can illuminate their path, guiding them towards their full potential.

"So, let us be the lightning to their fading flame, igniting their spirit and lighting up their journey with our faith in their abilities."

In topic conclusion:

In a world filled with **uncertainty and challenges,** practicing **"The Art of Believing"** can be a powerful tool to navigate through **life's ups and downs.**

Believing in oneself, in others, and in the possibilities that can cultivate a sense of hope and resilience. **It is about trusting in the process, having faith in the journey, and holding onto the belief that better days are yet to come.**

"Fight BackThrough Some Bad Days,

To Earn The Best Days of Your Life."

When we embrace **The Art of Believing,** we open ourselves up to endless opportunities and growth. It allows us to **dream big, set ambitious goals, and work towards turning our aspirations into reality.** Belief fuels passion, motivates action, and helps us push past obstacles that may come our way.

So, let us all embrace **The Art of Believing** – in ourselves, in each other, and in a brighter tomorrow. Together, we can create a world filled with positivity, possibility, and endless potential. **Remember,** practicing The Art of Believing is an ongoing journey.

"The more you actively cultivate and nurture your belief, the stronger it becomes."

Part B: Mastering "The Art of Believing" with The Subconscious Mind, Unleashing The Power Within

I. Introduction: The Power of the Subconscious Mind.

Mastering The Art of Believing through the influence of the subconscious mind is a powerful journey of **self-discovery** and **personal growth**. The subconscious mind holds immense power in shaping **our beliefs, thoughts, and actions.** To truly master this art, one must first understand the profound impact that our subconscious mind has on our daily lives.

By cultivating a **deep awareness of our thoughts and beliefs,** we can begin to harness **the power of the subconscious mind to manifest** our desires and aspirations. Through practices such as **visualization, positive affirmations, mindfulness, etc.** we can reprogram our subconscious mind to align with our true desires and intentions.

The key to mastering -The Art of Believing lies in **cultivating a strong sense of self-belief** and **unwavering faith in the power of our subconscious mind.** By tapping into this inner reservoir of strength and positivity, we can overcome challenges, manifest abundance, and create the life of our dreams.

Remember, The Art of Believing is not just about **wishful thinking;** it is about cultivating a deep sense of belief in oneself and the limitless potential of the subconscious mind.

With dedication, practice, and **a positive mindset,** you can unlock the secrets of the subconscious and harness its power to create the life you truly desire.

A. Explanation of the Subconscious Mind

The Subconscious mind plays a crucial role in practicing- "The Art of Believing". Our mind is a powerful tool that can either work for us or against us. Many of us are familiar with the concept of the conscious mind, the part of our brain that makes decisions and processes information in our waking state. However, there is another part of our mind that is equally powerful, yet often overlooked – **The Subconscious Mind.**

Understanding The Subconscious Mind

The subconscious mind is a part of our psyche that operates below the level of conscious awareness. It is responsible for storing all **the information gathered through our senses** and acts as a vast storage unit that holds all of **our past and present experiences, beliefs, emotions, memories, and habits.** This part of our mind works 24/7 and constantly working behind the scenes plays a crucial role in shaping **our personality and perception about ourselves and the world around us.**

Our subconscious mind influences **our thoughts, actions, behavior, and attitudes,** it is always active, even when we are not consciously aware of it, and plays a significant role in shaping **our thoughts, feelings, and actions.**

One of the **main characteristics** of the subconscious mind is that **it does not differentiate between reality and vivid imagination.** This means that the **beliefs and thoughts** we hold in our subconscious mind can have a powerful influence on our perception of reality and our reactions to different situations. **For instance,** if someone believes they are not good enough, this belief can manifest in their behavior and interactions, even if they are not consciously aware of it.

The subconscious mind is also responsible for controlling physical functions **such as breathing, heartbeat, and digestion,** as well as processing information at a rapid pace.

Remember, By understanding and working with our subconscious mind, we can work towards changing negative patterns and beliefs, and create a more positive and fulfilling life.

B. Importance of Understanding its Impact on Our Lives:

Delving into the subconscious mind is a complex and vast subject, but grasping its importance can lead to life-changing revelations and enhance purpose-driven life.

1. Self-awareness: Understanding the subconscious mind allows us to gain insight into our thoughts, behaviors, and beliefs that may be influencing our lives on a deeper level. By becoming more aware of our subconscious patterns, we can make more **informed choices and take control of our actions.**

2. Overcoming Limiting Beliefs: The subconscious mind is where many of **our limiting beliefs and self-sabotaging behaviors reside.** By understanding and addressing these beliefs, we can work towards overcoming obstacles that may be holding us back in various areas of our lives.

3. Improving Mental Health: Our subconscious mind can play a significant role in **our mental health, contributing to anxiety, depression, and other psychological issues.** By understanding how our subconscious mind impacts our emotions and behaviors, we can take steps toward improving our mental well-being.

4. Enhancing Personal Growth: Delving into the depths of our subconscious mind can **uncover hidden talents, strengths, and growth potential.** By exploring and understanding these aspects of ourselves, we can make positive changes and strive towards our full potential.

5. Strengthening Relationships: Our subconscious beliefs and emotions can influence **our interactions with others, often without us realizing it.** By gaining insight into how our subconscious mind impacts our relationships, we can improve communication, empathy, and connection with those around us.

Overall, **understanding the subconscious mind's impact on our lives** can lead to greater **self-awareness, personal growth, improved mental health, and stronger relationships.** By delving into the depths of our subconscious, we can unlock our true potential and lead more fulfilling and meaningful lives.

II. The Influence of the Subconscious Mind

The subconscious mind is a powerful force that plays a significant role in shaping our **thoughts, behaviors, and perceptions.** While the conscious mind deals with the **present moment and logical reasoning,** the subconscious mind operates behind the scenes, influencing **our beliefs, habits, and emotions.**

Understanding the influence of the subconscious mind can **lead to profound personal growth and transformation.** By becoming aware of the subconscious patterns and beliefs that drive our actions, we can begin to **make positive changes in our lives.**

Through practices such **as meditation, visualization, self-hypnosis, and affirmations,** we can access the power of the subconscious mind to manifest our goals and desires.

By **reprogramming our subconscious beliefs and replacing negative thought patterns with positive ones,** we can create a more fulfilling and meaningful life.

Ultimately, by harnessing the power of the subconscious mind, we can unlock our true potential and live a life of abundance, joy, and fulfillment.

A. How the Subconscious Mind Influences thoughts, emotions, and behaviors.

The power of the subconscious mind can greatly influence thoughts, emotions, and behaviors in various ways.

The following are ways in which our lives can be influenced by the subconscious mind:

1. Beliefs and perceptions:

The subconscious mind **holds deep-rooted beliefs and perceptions** that we may not even be aware of. These beliefs can shape our thoughts, emotions, and behaviors without realizing them.

For instance, if we believe that we are not worthy of success, this can manifest in **self-sabotaging behaviors and negative self-talk.** These limiting beliefs can create barriers to reaching our full potential and achieving our goals and aspirations. It is essential to recognize these patterns and work towards changing them. We can shift our mindset towards **self-worth and empowerment.**

"Remember, you are capable of achieving great things, and you deserve success just as much as anyone else. Embrace your worth and watch how it transforms your life for the better."

2. Emotional responses:

The subconscious mind is responsible for **our emotional responses** to various situations. It can trigger **feelings of anger, insecurities, doubts, fear, anxiety, or stress based on past experiences or traumas.**

These emotions can in turn influence **our thoughts and behaviors, leading to patterns of avoidance or self-destructive behavior.**

In previous chapters, we explored how emotions significantly influence, how we perceive the external world and shape our actions accordingly. Please refer back to that chapter for more details.

3. Habitual behaviors:

The subconscious mind is also responsible for **creating and maintaining habits.** These habits can be positive or negative, and they can have a significant impact on our daily lives. **For instance,** if we have a habit of **procrastinating,** this can be driven by subconscious beliefs or fears that can be hard to overcome without addressing them at a deeper level.

Imagine a person could show avoidance or irresponsible behavior in a situation or a circumstance or for others by continuously procrastinating important **tasks or responsibilities.** This behavior may stem from underlying **fears or anxiety about failure, rejection, or inadequacy.**

By **avoiding facing these challenges**, the person may **temporarily feel a sense of relief,** but in the long run, it can **lead to increased stress, missed opportunities, and a cycle of negative emotions.**

It's essential for individuals exhibiting avoidance or irresponsible behavior to explore the root causes of their actions, develop healthier coping mechanisms, and overcome these challenges.

When faced with challenging situations, it's important to recognize that avoidance, self-destructive, or irresponsible behavior are not sustainable solutions. **Instead, it's beneficial to face it with courage and resilience.**

Remember, By addressing the root causes of our struggles, we can work towards long-term healing and growth.

4. Memory and past experiences:

The subconscious mind **stores all of our memories and past experiences,** which can resurface in the form of **thoughts, emotions, and behaviors**.

These memories can trigger strong emotional responses or influence our decision-making process without our conscious realization of them.

For instance, a past traumatic experience can still impact our behavior and relationships years later. Overall, the subconscious mind holds immense power and can greatly influence our thoughts, emotions, and behaviors in ways that we may not even be aware of.

"The Subconscious Mind Acts As a Supportive Friend in Our Hard Times."

The truth of the subconscious mind quietly works behind the scenes, offering guidance and strength when we need it most. Our subconscious mind is like a loyal companion, always ready to provide comfort and reassurance in moments of uncertainty. By tapping into its wisdom, we can navigate through difficult situations with a sense of clarity and purpose.

Trust in your subconscious mind as a steadfast ally on your journey through life, knowing that it will always be there to offer solace and support whenever you need it. When you find yourself alone or feeling down, try talking to your inner companion. It can guide you during challenging times. Just as a trusted friend offers support and encouragement, your subconscious mind can provide insights and wisdom when you most need it. By engaging in self-talk and introspection, you can tap into this invaluable resource within you.

Remember, the power of the subconscious mind lies in its ability to navigate your emotions and thoughts, offering a sense of clarity and comfort even amid difficulty. So, next time you feel overwhelmed or lost, turn to your inner companion for guidance and reassurance. Trust in its ability to help you navigate through life's challenges with strength and resilience.

B. How the Subconscious Mind influences decision-making.

The power of the subconscious mind can greatly impact decision-making by influencing **thoughts, beliefs, and actions** on a subconscious level.

Here are some ways in which the subconscious mind can influence decision-making:

1. Intuition and gut feelings:

The subconscious mind can **send signals to the conscious mind through intuition or gut feelings that guide decision-making.** These feelings are often based on past experiences, instincts, and emotions stored in the subconscious mind.

For instance, when faced with a difficult choice, our intuition might nudge us in a certain direction based on patterns it has recognized from similar situations in the past. This **intuitive guidance can be a powerful tool in helping us make decisions** that align with our values and goals, even when we may not have all the information at hand.

Trusting our intuition and listening to our gut feelings can lead us down a path that feels right for us, even if it may not always be the **most logical choice on the surface.**

Embracing these subtle signals from our subconscious mind can help us navigate life's uncertainties with more clarity and confidence.

2. Beliefs and biases:

Our beliefs and biases, which are formed in the subconscious mind, can heavily influence the decisions we make. These beliefs may be based on societal norms, personal experiences, or cultural influences that shape our perception of reality.

3. Fear and self-doubt:

Negative emotions such as **fear, self-doubt, and anxiety** stored in the subconscious mind can lead to **indecision, hesitation, or avoidance** of **making tough decisions.** These emotions may block us from taking risks or stepping out of **our comfort zones.**

4. Habits and patterns:

The subconscious mind is responsible for forming habits and patterns that dictate our **behaviors and choices.** These automatic responses can result in making d**ecisions without conscious thought or consideration.**

5. Visualization and manifestation:

The subconscious mind is powerful in visualizing outcomes and manifesting our desires. By harnessing the power of positive affirmations, visualization techniques, and goal-setting, we can reprogram our subconscious mind to support us in making decisions that align with our goals and aspirations.

Overall, the power of the subconscious mind plays a significant role in **decision-making by influencing our thoughts, beliefs, emotions, and behaviors.**

By becoming aware of these subconscious influences and actively working to reprogram them, we can make more **informed, intentional, and empowered decisions** in our daily lives.

C. How the subconscious mind plays a crucial role in shaping our beliefs and perceptions.

The subconscious mind plays a crucial role in shaping our beliefs and perceptions. Our subconscious mind is like a powerful tape recorder that stores all of our **past experiences, memories, and beliefs,** and uses them **to shape how we view the world and ourselves.**

Our subconscious mind is constantly working behind the scenes to filter and interpret the vast amount of information that we are bombarded with daily. It acts as a kind of personal assistant, sorting through the information and deciding **what is important and what can be ignored.**

One suggestion, You can understand more about how our subconscious mind operates behind the scenes by watching the **Disney movie "Inside Out."** The film illustrates how our mind continuously processes information in the background, showcasing the intricate mechanisms of information processing.

One of the key ways that the subconscious **mind shapes our beliefs** and **perceptions** is **through repetition.** When we are exposed to **the same information or idea over and over again,** our subconscious mind **begins to accept it as true,** even if it may not necessarily be accurate.

This is why advertising works so well - by repeatedly bombarding us with messages about a product or brand, our subconscious mind begins to believe that it is desirable and trustworthy.

Our subconscious mind also plays a role in **forming our self-image and beliefs** about ourselves. If we have been repeatedly told or shown that we are not good enough, smart enough, or capable enough, our subconscious mind will internalize these beliefs and hold us back from reaching our full potential.

Our subconscious mind plays a crucial role in **shaping our beliefs, perceptions, and personality because it stores all of our past and present experiences, memories, and emotions.** These stored thoughts and feelings can influence how we perceive and interpret new information and situations.

For instance, if we had negative experiences in the past, our subconscious mind may create a belief that similar situations will also be negative. This can lead to **a pessimistic outlook on life and cloud our judgments about new experiences.**

Similarly, our subconscious mind can also shape **our beliefs about ourselves.** If we have internalized negative feedback or experiences in the past, our subconscious mind may create a belief that we are not good enough or deserving of success.

By becoming aware of our subconscious beliefs and perceptions and By changing our subconscious thought process, we can ultimately change our beliefs and perceptions, leading to a more positive and fulfilling life.

In Topic Conclusion:

This topic emphasizes how our subconscious mind has a significant impact on our daily lives.

"Our thoughts, words, and actions, play a role in shaping who we are as individuals."

By being mindful of the information we absorb through various channels (visualization, auditory cues, or verbal means), we can better understand how our subconscious mind processes and influences our **thoughts, behaviors, and perceptions.**

Our subconscious mind **absorbs and processes** every piece of information and influences in our daily lives. This awareness empowers us **to take control of our thoughts and actions, leading to personal growth and positive change.**

Remember, our subconscious mind holds immense power, and by harnessing it for goodness, we can create a more fulfilling and enriched life.

"Make Sure To Be A Good Teacher For Yourself".

Take a Closer Look and Imagine: The conscious mind plays the role of a teacher, instructing what to do, whereas the subconscious mind acts as a student, following those instructions promptly.

It's a well-known fact that a good teacher instills good interests and habits in their student. Remember, the importance of selecting teaching content wisely for yourself by absorbing high-quality information through your senses.

Allow your subconscious to absorb beneficial teachings and improve your performance. As a teacher, it's your responsibility to teach your mind well and correct the mistakes when necessary.

Your teaching should be effective and help the mind to enhance learning and performance. However, it's equally important to be strict when necessary and firmly correct your mistakes. By doing so, you not only help your mind to avoid repeating the same mistakes but also prepare for the challenges it may face in the future.

III. Subconscious Mind and Self-Sabotage

A. Understanding Self-Sabotage Behavior.

Self-sabotage behavior refers to the **actions, thoughts, or behaviors that prevent an individual from achieving their goals or fulfilling their potential.** This **destructive behavior** is often driven by **underlying psychological issues** such as **low self-esteem, fear of failure, lack of self-confidence, or past traumas.**

Some common examples of **self-sabotage behavio**r include **procrastination, negative self-talk, perfectionism, self-doubt, avoidance of challenges,** and **self-destructive habits such as excessive drinking or substance abuse.** These behaviors can manifest in various aspects of life, such as **relationships, careers, health, and personal development.**

It is important to identify and understand **self-sabotage behavior** to address and overcome it. This can involve seeking therapy or counseling to **uncover the root causes of these destructive patterns, developing healthier coping mechanisms and strategies for managing stress and negative emotions, setting realistic goals and expectations, and practicing self-care and self-compassion.**

By **recognizing and addressing self-sabotage behavior,** individuals can work towards **breaking free from self-limiting beliefs and patterns,** and ultimately achieving their full potential and leading a more fulfilling and successful life.

B. How the subconscious mind contributes to self-sabotage.

The subconscious mind **plays a significant role in self-sabotage** as it is part of our minds. It is responsible for **storing deeply ingrained beliefs, memories, and patterns of behavior that influence our thoughts, feelings, and actions.**

One way in which the subconscious mind contributes to **self-sabotage is through negative self-talk and limiting beliefs.** These beliefs are often formed in childhood based on **past experiences, traumas, or messages from authority figures.** When these beliefs **are not challenged or changed,** they continue to **dictate our behaviors and decisions.**

For instance, if someone has a belief that they are not good enough, they may consistently undermine their own **success or relationships by procrastinating, self-sabotaging, or engaging in self-destructive behaviors.**

Additionally, the subconscious mind can also **create resistance to change and growth.** This can manifest as fear of the unknown, fear of failure, or fear of success. When we resist stepping outside of our comfort zones or taking risks, we stay stuck in patterns of self-sabotage that prevent us from reaching our full potential.

To overcome self-sabotage, it is important to **identify and challenge the negative beliefs and patterns stored in the subconscious mind.** This may **require therapy, self-reflection, and mindfulness practices to uncover and reprogram these thoughts and behaviors.**

By becoming more aware of how the subconscious mind contributes to **self-sabotage,** we can take steps to **change**

our mindset and create more positive and empowering beliefs that support our goals, aspirations, and long-term growth.

Remember, it's never too late to rewrite the story you tell yourself and create a more empowering narrative for a brighter future.

C. Techniques to overcome self-sabotage through reprogramming the subconscious mind.

The methods to **combat self-sabotage by reprogramming the subconscious mind** are already outlined in the preceding chapter. In summary, **here are a few key points for a quick view.**

1. Identify negative beliefs and thought patterns: Become aware of the negative beliefs and thought patterns that are holding you back from reaching your goals.

2. Challenge and reframe negative beliefs: Consciously challenge negative beliefs and reframe them into more positive and empowering beliefs. For instance, if you believe you are not good enough, reframe it to "I am capable and deserving of success."

3. Visualization and affirmations: Use visualization and positive affirmations to reprogram your subconscious mind. Visualize yourself already achieving your goals and use positive affirmations to reinforce this belief.

4. Hypnosis and guided meditation: Consider using hypnosis or guided meditation to access the subconscious mind and reprogram it with positive beliefs and thoughts.

5. Practice mindfulness and self-awareness: Develop a regular mindfulness practice to bring awareness to your thoughts and behaviors. By being more conscious of your subconscious patterns, you can change them.

6. Set clear goals and take action: Set clear, achievable goals and consistently act towards reaching them. By progressing towards your goals, you will build confidence and belief in yourself.

7. Seek support from a therapist or coach: Consider seeking support from a therapist or coach who can help you identify and overcome self-sabotaging behaviors. They can provide guidance and tools to help reprogram your subconscious mind.

IV. Reprogram the Subconscious Mind:

In today's world, managing our thoughts has become challenging due to the overwhelming amount of information we encounter. This sensory overload makes it hard for us to concentrate on different areas of our lives. We often rush through activities like eating, talking, and working on different tasks, unintentionally endangering our life's path.

Now we understand that our subconscious mind operates in the background, absorbing information from our senses without our awareness and shaping our personality, whether positively or negatively. It is crucial to select our content carefully to mirror our desired persona. To address these concerns, we need to reprogram your subconscious mind by replacing negative content with positive one and by **altering the beliefs, thoughts, and behavior patterns stored in the subconscious mind.**

Initially, our subconscious mind **develops its programming** through our past experiences, childhood upbringing, societal and cultural conditioning, and repeating patterns of behavior, bombarding with pieces of information. However, **this programming may only sometimes be supportive or beneficial to our personal growth and well-being.**

The good news is that we can transform negative patterns by reprogramming your subconscious mind. **Remember, Our mind holds incredible power and features a delete option. We can eliminate undesired elements and paint a magnificent picture as we desire.**

A. Reprogramming the Subconscious Mind:

Reprogramming the subconscious mind refers to **the process of changing the deeply rooted beliefs, patterns, and behaviors that are stored in the subconscious mind.** As we know, The subconscious mind plays a crucial role in **influencing our thoughts, emotions, and actions on a daily basis.**

Reprogramming the subconscious mind **involves consciously identifying and replacing old limiting beliefs, negative thought patterns, and unhelpful behaviors with new, positive, and empowering ones.**

This can be achieved through **various techniques such as affirmations, visualization, hypnosis, meditation, and other practices** that aim to access and **influence the subconscious mind positively** to have desired outcomes.

Reprogramming is like **decluttering our minds.** Just as we tidy our homes daily, or during the festive season, we embark on a thorough clean. Occasionally, deep cleaning is necessary, especially if the stains are stubborn. Seeking assistance might be required. It can be time-consuming, energy-draining, and even frustrating. However, the effort is worthwhile as the end goal is to have a beautiful and elegant home, isn't it?

Similarly, reprogramming our subconscious mind **requires patience, conscious awareness, and long-term dedication.** It's like **being a farmer, tending to the garden, and consistently removing weeds.** It's a gradual process of nurturing positive thoughts, beliefs, and habits while gently uprooting any negative patterns that no longer serve us.

Just as a farmer tends to the soil, planting seeds of positivity and watering them with positive affirmations and self-care rituals, we too must cultivate our minds with **mindfulness and self-compassion.** Over time, with patience and persistence, we can transform our subconscious landscape into a fertile ground for growth, resilience, and inner peace.

B. Understanding the Importance of Reprogramming the Subconscious Mind.

Reprogramming the subconscious mind is important because it plays a significant role in shaping **our beliefs, behaviors, and attitudes.** Our subconscious mind is like **a tape recorder** that stores all of **our past experiences, thoughts, and emotions.** This programming influences **our thoughts and behavior** daily, often **without us even realizing it.**

By reprogramming the subconscious mind, we can **overwrite negative beliefs and patterns that may be holding us back.** This can help us **break free from limiting beliefs, overcome fears and insecurities, anger and outbursts,** and **create new, positive habits, and highly elevated emotions** that align with our purpose-driven lives.

By reprogramming the subconscious mind, individuals **can work towards positive changes, overcome self-sabotaging behaviors, enhance self-confidence, improve relationships, and achieve personal goals and aspirations.** It is believed that by aligning the subconscious mind with one's desires and objectives, individuals can manifest their **aspirations and create** a more fulfilling and successful life.

Reprogramming the subconscious mind can also help **improve mental and emotional well-being, as it can reduce stress, anxiety, and negative thought patterns.** It can also improve **self-esteem, confidence, and overall happiness** by creating a **more positive and empowering internal dialogue.**

Overall, reprogramming the subconscious mind is important for **personal growth and development,** as it allows us to **take control of our thoughts and beliefs,** and ultimately create a more joyful and successful life.

Some approaches commonly used to reprogram the subconscious Mind: Below are some methods to reprogram the subconscious mind, which we will explore further in an upcoming chapter, The Techniques of Practicing Art of Believing.

Positive Affirmations, Use positive statements, such as "I am confident and capable," repeatedly to replace negative self-talk and rewire the subconscious mind over time.

Visualization: Creating vivid mental images of desired outcomes and repeatedly visualizing them can help reprogram the subconscious mind to align with those goals and aspirations.

Hypnosis: Utilizing hypnotherapy techniques to access the subconscious mind and implant new suggestions and beliefs.

Neuro-Linguistic Programming (NLP): NLP techniques involve reprogramming the subconscious mind by using language patterns and specific techniques to create rapid changes in behavior and thought patterns.

In Topic conclusion:

Once you decide to declutter your mind, you will pave the way to achieving your goals and aspirations. It's crucial to release anything that no longer serves you. Imagine this, just as you can perceive others' energy and thoughts, you can also project your energy and thoughts to them with deliberate intent!

Remember, You hold the pen to script your destiny, jump out from the bed or a couch, begin today by mapping out your journey, and look back every five years. Appreciate and embrace how the beauty of your flourishing garden is filled with the sweet fragrance of flowers and fruits. Stay joyful and embrace the exciting chapters ahead.

V. Techniques for Practicing "The Art of Believing"

Practicing **"The Art of Believing"** Techniques involves letting go of outdated limiting beliefs and thoughts that no longer serve a purpose in our lives, similar to **decluttering unnecessary items and believing in your inner potential.**

By releasing these old beliefs, we create space for new, empowering beliefs to take root and flourish within us. Just like decluttering a room allows for a fresh perspective and a sense of renewal, letting go of limiting beliefs can open up endless possibilities for growth and success.

Embracing the art of believing in ourselves and our inner potential can lead to a fulfilling and purposeful life. Trust in your abilities, have faith in your journey and watch as your belief in yourself propels you to new heights of accomplishment and happiness.

Here are some Techniques for Practicing "The Art of Believing".

1. Visualization:

Visualization is a powerful **mental technique that involves creating detailed and vivid mental images onto the screen of our subconscious mind of** your desired outcomes, goals, or aspirations. Our subconscious mind cannot differentiate between reality and vivid imagination. When we visualize our dreams and visions with clarity and detail, our subconscious mind **perceives them as real experiences.**

How Visualisation reprograms the subconscious mind

Visualization can help to **reprogram our beliefs and attitudes,** making it easier for us to achieve what we desire.

Visualization can reprogram the subconscious mind by repetitively exposing it to positive images, thoughts, and scenarios. When we consistently visualize our desired outcomes or behaviors, we create neural pathways in our brains that reinforce those thoughts and beliefs. Over time, this can lead to changes in behavior, attitudes, and beliefs, as your subconscious mind begins to accept these visualized scenarios as reality. It's like training your mind to focus on what you want to achieve, which can lead to greater confidence, motivation, and ultimately, success.

By **regularly visualizing** our goals and aspirations, **we can create a strong connection between our conscious and subconscious minds,** ultimately leading us toward success and fulfillment. **So, take some time each day to visualize your aspirations and watch as your subconscious mind works tirelessly to bring them to life.**

When **practicing visualization,** it's important to engage all your senses to **make the experience as real and immersive as possible.** Imagine not just what achieving your goal would look like, but also how it would feel, sound, smell, and even taste.

By incorporating all your senses, you can make your visualizations more impactful and increase the likelihood of manifesting your dreams into reality. **Remember, the mind is a powerful tool, and visualization can help you harness that power to create the life you desire.**

Let's engage in a practical exercise. Take a moment to visualize – wherever you are, close your eyes and picture yourself in your kitchen. Slowly approach the refrigerator, open it gently, and take out a fresh orange. Peel it, put a piece in your mouth, and feel it, does it savor the taste? If you feel a sense of delight, you are moving in the right direction towards visualizing your goals and aspirations. If not, don't feel discouraged; keep practicing. You'll get there.

Exploring the Visualization Techniques: Visualization requires continuous practice and dedication for desired outcomes and long-term results.

To enhance your visualization skills, consider the following key points:

1. **Clarity:** Clearly define what you want to visualize. The more specific and detailed your mental image, the more effective it will be.

2. **Engage All Senses:** Try to involve all your senses in the visualization. Imagine not only what you would see but also what you would hear, smell, taste, and feel in that situation.

3. **Emotion:** Attach positive emotions to your visualization. Feel the joy, excitement, and satisfaction associated with achieving your goal.

4. **Repetition:** Practice visualization regularly. Make it a daily habit to reinforce your belief in your goals.

5. **Belief:** As you visualize, truly believe that what you're imagining is possible and attainable.

6. **Realism:** While you want to be positive, keep your visualizations realistic. Visualizing something entirely beyond your capabilities may lead to frustration.

7. **Use Visualization Scripts:** Some people find it helpful to follow a written script or guided visualization audio to get started.

8. Quiet Environment: Find a quiet and comfortable place to practice visualization, free from distractions.

9. Mental Rehearsal: Use visualization as a mental rehearsal for challenging situations. It can boost your confidence and performance in real-life scenarios.

10. Combine with Action: Visualization is most effective when paired with action. After visualizing your goals, take concrete steps toward achieving them.

Remember that visualization is a **tool to reinforce belief and motivation.** It can help align your **thoughts, emotions, and actions** with your goals, ultimately increasing your chances of success.

Let's Embark on Dolly's Journey: How Visualization Techniques Led to Riya's Birth.

Dolly, like any other ordinary girl, dreamt about her future married life, how she would navigate it, and what comes after. During her college years, she fell in love and planned to marry after finishing her education. She completed her studies and tied the knot.

During her romantic relationship, Dolly expressed her desire to have a daughter, whom she named Riya. She enthusiastically spoke about Riya to her partner and friends, envisioning her as a real person. She detailed Riya's characteristics, behaviors, and reactions towards her mom.

In her spare moments amid her college studies and busy schedules, Dolly imagined Riya as her future daughter – picturing her appearance and personality. She would vividly describe Riya's personality, actions, appearance, and how she would protect her mother. Interestingly, her friends saved her contact number as Riya even before the child's birth.

Like any other bride, Dolly had a grand wedding. A year later, she became pregnant and she welcomed and gave birth to a beautiful baby girl. **Dolly was** Overwhelmed with joy, she realized that her nine years of visualization had manifested into a tangible miracle. When she announces the arrival of her baby to her family and friends, they realize, **"Oh, Riya has arrived."** Everyone congratulated and celebrated as the daydream came to life. Everyone **marveled at the miracle.**

Her story serves as a testament to **the power of visualization and manifestation** in our lives. Dolly's journey highlights how the practice of visualizing her desired future helped bring about the birth of her daughter Riya.

"No matter how long it may take to materialize, I want you to know that anything is possible."

Here are some key takeaways from Dolly's story:

Clarity of Vision: Dolly had a clear vision of **what she wanted in her future,** specifically visualizing her daughter Riya's **personality, actions, appearance, and their relationship.** This clarity helped solidify her intentions and desires.

Consistent Practice: Dolly didn't just visualize once and forget about it; she **dedicated nine years to consistently imagining and manifesting** her dream of having a daughter named Riya. This consistent practice kept her focused on her goal.

Emotional Connection: Dolly not only visualized Riya's **physical attributes but also emotional qualities** like how her daughter would defend her. This emotional connection added depth to her visualizations and strengthened her bond with the idea of Riya.

Supportive Environment: Dolly's friends also played a role in her journey by saving her contact with the name Riya before the child's birth. This supportive environment helped reinforce Dolly's vision and belief in the manifestation process.

Belief in the Outcome: Ultimately, **Dolly's unwavering belief in the power of visualization and manifestation** led to the realization of her dream when she welcomed Riya into the world. Her story underscores the importance of believing in the outcome we visualize.

Dolly's story is a reminder that our thoughts and intentions have the power to shape our reality. By harnessing the practice of visualization and maintaining a positive mindset, we can work towards manifesting our dreams, goals, and aspirations in life.

"Visualization is daydreaming with a purpose. Dare to do daydreams. Proud to be a dreamer."

2. Positive affirmation

Positive affirmation is a statement or phrase that is used to reinforce positive thoughts and beliefs. It is commonly used in **self-help, self-empowerment, and personal development to cultivate a positive mindset, build self-confidence, overcome self-limiting beliefs, and empower relationships.**

How do affirmations reprogram the subconscious mind?

Affirmations allow to instill positive beliefs and reprogram the subconscious mind. By consistently **repeating affirmations,** individuals can **reinforce desired thoughts and feelings,** which helps to create **new neural pathways in the brain.**

This repetition helps to replace negative or **limiting beliefs** that may be held in the subconscious mind with more positive and empowering beliefs. Over time, the subconscious mind begins to **accept these new beliefs as truth,** leading to **changes in behavior, emotions, and overall mindset.**

In essence, **affirmations work to challenge and override long-held beliefs and patterns of thinking by consistently reinforcing new, positive messages.** By engaging with affirmations regularly and with intention, individuals can effectively reprogram their subconscious mind to align with their desired outcomes and goals.

Repeated positive affirmations are declarations about yourself and your abilities. Over time, these affirmations will become a **drill in your subconscious mind, reinforcing your belief in yourself.** With each **positive declaration,** you cultivate a mindset that empowers you to face challenges with courage and determination. The more **you repeat these affirmations,** the more they **take root in your subconscious, positively shaping your thoughts and actions.**

By repeatedly **affirming positive statements,** individuals **aim to replace negative thoughts and patterns with empowering and constructive ones. Positive affirmations** may include statements such as **"I am worthy," "I am capable of achieving my goals," or "I attract positive experiences into my life."**

As we continue to practice **positive self-affirmations, we are nurturing a garden of self-belief within us.** Each affirmation **acts as a seed, planted in the fertile soil of your mind, growing stronger and more resilient with every repetition.** Just like **a gardener tends to their plants with care and attention,** you are nurturing a mindset of **confidence and self-worth.**

So, Keep nurturing these seeds of positivity and watch as they blossom into a beautiful garden of self-assurance and inner strength.

"Remember, you are the architect of your self-belief, and with each affirmation, you are building a strong foundation of confidence that will support you on your journey toward success."

Practice Some Positive Affirmation: Positive Statements In Your Daily Life.

"I am enough, and I have everything within me to achieve my goals."

"I deserve love and happiness in my life."

"I am confident and capable of handling

any challenges that come my way."

"I am resilient and can bounce back from any setback."

"I am worthy of success and prosperity."

"I am surrounded by love, positivity, and abundance."

"I am grateful for all the blessings and opportunities in my life."

"I am proud of who I am and how far I have come."

"I choose to focus on the positive and let go of negativity."

"I am deserving of self-care, self-love, and self-compassion."

“Positive Affirmation on Health”

“Every day, in every way, I am getting healthier and stronger."

"I nourish my body with healthy, wholesome foods that promote optimal health."

"I am grateful for my vibrant, energetic body and take good care of it."

"I radiate good health, vitality, and inner peace."

"I am in perfect harmony with my body's natural healing abilities."

"My body is a temple, and I treat it with love and respect."

"I choose to prioritize my health and make positive choices for my well-being."

"I am worthy of vibrant health, and I align my thoughts and actions accordingly."

"I release all stress and tension from my body, allowing it to heal and thrive."

"I am grateful for my body's remarkable abilities and support its well-being with regular exercise and rest."

Spiritual Affirmation on Health.

If you are experiencing any doubt or sickness, it might be either psychological or physiological. Embrace these affirmations to lead a healthy and stress-free life.

I affirm that my body is a sacred vessel of divine energy and vitality. Each day, I radiate vibrant health and well-being. I am grateful for the miraculous healing power that courses through my being, restoring and revitalizing every cell and organ. I honor and nurture my body with nourishment, exercise, and self-care.

I release any fear or doubt that may hinder my well-being and embrace the inherent strength within me. I trust in the wisdom of my body, knowing that it carries the innate ability to heal itself. I surround myself with loving, supportive energies that uplift and inspire my wellness journey. I manifest divine love and light, and as I align with this truth, perfect health flows effortlessly into my life.

I gratefully embrace the gift of health, and with gratitude, I fervently declare that I am whole, healthy, and divine in every way.

Oh, my “Heavenly Father” accepts my prayer and fills me with your divinity.

Let's take a moment and appreciate how Sulochana Oguri, utilized positive affirmations to free herself from mental darkness and confusion, that led her to fall into negative and catastrophic thinking.

In her life, Sulochna Oguri faced medical challenges that required hospital investigations like MRI scanning. Throughout the period, she felt anxious due to the MRI machine noises, fear of surgery, lockdown circumstances due to the pandemic, COVID testing, hospitalization, and more.

Sulochna's fear and anxiety were strongly rooted in her subconscious mind and kept her up at night for months. Engulfed her in catastrophic thoughts such as doubts about her survival, imaginary threats, and feeling isolated. She remained in a state of sleepless nights and catastrophic thoughts for an extended time.

Despite her struggles, she found it hard to express her feelings to her family. She wanted to seek help from a psychiatrist for her betterment, but she wasn't. Additionally, she grappled with the fear of societal judgment, She felt trapped, worrying about the social stigma associated with seeking mental health treatment.

She was unsure of what to do next and felt completely lost in the situation, feeling stranded in an ocean of despair where no one had heard her cries or offered a way out of the perilous situation. In the middle of the suffering, she heard an inner call for positive affirmations and spiritual practice.

Sulochana found herself in a challenging situation. However, Sulochna listens to her inner voice and she has turned her mind to positive affirmations and spiritual practices to shift her mindset away from negativity.

As she embarked on a journey of transformation, transitioning from negative thoughts to a positive mindset through affirmations and spiritual practices, her subconscious mind played a crucial role in reshaping her past traumatic experiences into uplifting ones. This transformative process wasn't quick; it took two years to replace her old negative memories with positive ones. Now she fully recovered, leading a healthy life from the catastrophic thinking.

She demonstrated that by practicing positive affirmations and spiritual practices, anyone can reprogram their subconscious mind and break free from negative thoughts, and limiting beliefs.

Her story inspired many to embrace their healing journey and find the strength within to conquer their inner demons. Through her resilience and determination, she showed that **the power of positivity and self-love can truly transform lives.** As she continued to thrive and spread her message of hope, she became a beacon of light for those seeking their own path to healing and happiness.

With patience and dedication, she slowly unraveled the layers of negativity that had once clouded her vision. As she immersed herself in spiritual practices that resonated with her soul, she found solace in the beauty of the present moment and the limitless possibilities that lay ahead.

Her journey was a testament to the transformative power of self-love and belief in the inherent goodness within. With each passing day, she grew stronger, more radiant, and more aligned with her true purpose. Her story served as a beacon of hope for all who sought to rewrite their own narratives and embrace a life filled with boundless positivity and light.

3. Forgiveness

Forgiveness is a conscious decision to let go of feelings of anger, resentment, or bitterness towards someone who has hurt or wronged you. It is a willingness to move beyond the hurt and embrace a sense of peace and freedom.

Forgiveness does not mean forgetting or excusing the other person's actions, but rather it is a powerful act of self-healing and liberation. By forgiving others, we can release ourselves from **the burden of carrying around negative emotions** and **create space for love, understanding, and compassion in our hearts.**

How forgiveness reprograms the subconscious mind.

Forgiveness can reprogram the subconscious mind by releasing negative emotions and limiting beliefs that are stored in the subconscious. When we forgive others or ourselves, we let go of anger, resentment, and other negative emotions that can create blocks in our subconscious mind. This allows us to replace those negative thoughts and beliefs with more positive and empowering ones.

Forgiveness also helps to rewire the brain, creating new neural pathways that support healthier thought patterns and behaviors. By **repeatedly practicing forgiveness,** we can train our subconscious mind to **respond to situations** more **positively and compassionately.**

Overall, forgiveness can help to reprogram the subconscious mind by **clearing out old emotional baggage** and **creating space for new**, more positive beliefs and attitudes to take root. This can lead to a more peaceful and fulfilling life.

For instance, let's say someone **has been holding onto a grudge against a friend for years after they did something hurtful.** Every time they think about that friend or the situation, they feel anger and resentment bubbling up inside them. This negative energy is stored in their subconscious mind, affecting their thoughts, emotions, and behavior in various aspects of their life.

If this person chooses to forgive their friend and let go of the grudge, they are freeing themselves from the negative energy that has been weighing them down. By releasing this burden, they are reprogramming their subconscious mind to let go of anger and bitterness, making room for more positive thoughts and emotions to thrive.

Forgiveness allows us **to make peace with the past, heal old wounds, and move forward with a renewed sense of clarity, positivity, and empowerment.** By **practicing forgiveness regularly,** we can create a more positive and healthy subconscious mind that is free from the burdens of the past and open to new possibilities and growth.

How to practice forgiveness:

3. 1 Acknowledge your feelings: Start by recognizing and accepting the hurt or anger you may be feeling. It's essential to acknowledge your emotions before you can begin the process of forgiveness.

3. 2 Understand the situation: Try to see things from the other person's perspective. Understanding their actions or motivations can help you empathize and move toward forgiveness.

3. 3 Let go of resentment: Holding onto resentment only harms you in the long run. Practice letting go of negative feelings and focus on healing yourself.

3. 4 Communicate your feelings: If you feel comfortable, consider discussing your feelings with the person who hurt you. Honest communication can help facilitate the forgiveness process.

3. 5 Practice self-care: Forgiveness is a process that takes time and effort. Make sure to take care of yourself along the way, whether it's through **self-reflection, therapy, or engaging in activities that bring you joy.**

3. 6 Be patient with yourself: Forgiveness is not always easy, and it's okay to take your time. Be patient with yourself as you navigate through your emotions and work towards letting go of resentment.

Remember, forgiveness is a powerful tool that can bring peace and healing into your life. By practicing forgiveness, you can release yourself from the burden of anger and move towards a more positive and fulfilling future.

"Life is like an adventure, full of ups and downs, just like a rollercoaster ride."

It's always advisable to travel light to have a smoother and more enjoyable journey. During our lifetime, we come across various people in different situations. Some of them offer us support while others teach us valuable lessons. Supportive encounters become cherished memories while lessons learned can be tough experiences. By facing challenges with integrity and embracing both aspects of life, we can progress through different stages and eventually reach our destination.

"Forgiveness is like letting go of emotional baggage that is no longer necessary and enjoying a peaceful life's journey"

4. Gratitude

Practicing gratitude is a powerful way to reprogram the subconscious mind. By focusing on what you're thankful for, you shift your mindset towards positivity and abundance. This can help rewire your brain to notice and appreciate the good things in your life, leading to increased happiness, resilience, and overall well-being. Incorporating gratitude into your daily routine through journaling, reflection, or simply expressing appreciation to others can have profound effects on your subconscious mind and overall outlook on life.

How Gratitude Reprograms the Subconscious Mind.

Gratitude reprograms the subconscious mind by **shifting your focus from negative thoughts and emotions to positive ones.** When you consistently express gratitude for the things you have, **you train your subconscious mind to recognize and appreciate abundance rather than scarcity.** This repetitive practice strengthens **neural pathways** associated with positive emotions and fosters a mindset of optimism and contentment. Over time, your subconscious mind internalizes these positive beliefs, leading to a more resilient, fulfilled, and optimistic outlook on life.

Gratitude can reprogram your subconscious mind in a few ways:

4.1 Focus on the positive: By practicing gratitude, we train our minds to focus on the positive aspects of our lives. This shifts our perspective from one of lack and negativity to one of abundance and appreciation.

4.2 Attract more positivity: Gratitude creates a positive energy that attracts more positive experiences and opportunities into our lives. By focusing on what we are grateful for, we are more likely to notice and attract even more things to be grateful for.

4.3 Shift limiting beliefs: Gratitude can help us challenge and shift limiting beliefs that may be holding us back. By acknowledging and appreciating the good things in our lives, we can start to see new possibilities and potential for growth and change.

4.4 Increase resilience: Practicing gratitude can also help us build resilience and cope with challenges more effectively. When we focus on what we are grateful for, we strengthen our ability to stay positive and optimistic in the face of adversity.

Overall, gratitude can help reprogram our subconscious minds by creating a more positive, optimistic, and abundant mindset that can transform our lives for the better.

"Shifting our focus from what's wrong to what's right is an ultimate choice "

This change in perspective leads to gratitude, which is essential for happiness. This quote emphasizes that gratitude is the path to joy and prompts us to appreciate the positive aspects of our lives.

5. Self-hypnosis

Self-hypnosis is a technique in which an individual induces a hypnotic state on their own, without the assistance of a hypnotist or therapist. It involves using various methods such as **relaxation techniques, guided visualization, and positive affirmations** to achieve a trance-like state and access the subconscious mind. It is often used for **self-improvement, stress reduction, behavior modification, and enhancing mental and physical well-being.**

Self-hypnosis is a technique that allows individuals to enter a state of deep relaxation and focused attention to access their subconscious mind and make positive changes in thoughts, feelings, and behaviors.

This can be achieved through the use of **self-guided scripts, visualizations, and affirmations, as well as techniques such as deep breathing and progressive muscle relaxation.** Self-hypnosis can be a powerful tool for overcoming fears and phobias, managing stress and anxiety, improving confidence and self-esteem, and enhancing performance in various areas of life. It is important to approach self-hypnosis with an open mind and a willingness to practice regularly to see results.

How does self-hypnosis reprogram the subconscious mind?

Self-hypnosis can reprogram the subconscious mind by inducing a state of deep relaxation and heightened suggestibility. During self-hypnosis, you can access your subconscious mind more directly and suggest positive affirmations, beliefs, or behaviors to yourself. By repeatedly exposing your subconscious mind to these suggestions while in a relaxed state, you can gradually replace negative or limiting beliefs with more empowering ones. Over time, this process can lead to profound changes in attitudes, behaviors, and perceptions as your subconscious mind begins to accept and integrate these new suggestions as reality.

6. Creating a vision board:

Visualizing your goals and desires can be a powerful way to reprogram your subconscious mind. **A vision board is a tangible representation** of your dreams and aspirations. By compiling **images, quotes, and symbols** that resonate with your deepest desires, you are sending a clear message to your subconscious about what you want to manifest in your life.

Place your vision board somewhere you will see it every day, allowing these positive affirmations to seep into your subconscious and guide your actions toward achieving your goals. **Remember, the more you immerse yourself in your vision board, the more your subconscious mind will start aligning your thoughts and actions with your intentions.**

Creating a vision board can be a wonderful way to manifest your dreams and goals. Start by gathering materials such as **magazines, photos, quotes, and other items** that inspire you. Find a quiet space where you can focus and let your creativity flow. As you arrange your chosen items on the board, visualize your aspirations coming to life. Be sure to include a mix of short-term and long-term goals, and don't be afraid to dream big.

Your vision board is a reflection of your inner desires and can serve as a powerful tool to keep you motivated and on track toward achieving your dreams. **Enjoy the process and have fun bringing your vision to life!**

How does the vision board reprogram the subconscious mind?

A vision board reprograms the subconscious mind by providing a visual representation of your goals, desires, and aspirations. When you create a vision board, you select images, words, and symbols that represent what you want to achieve or manifest in your life. By regularly viewing your vision board, you immerse your subconscious mind in these positive visualizations, reinforcing your goals and desires.

The consistent exposure to your vision board helps to activate the reticular activating system (RAS) in your brain, which filters and prioritizes information based on your goals and intentions. This means that your subconscious mind becomes more attuned to opportunities, resources, and experiences that align with what you've depicted on your vision board.

Additionally, the act of creating and maintaining a vision board can evoke positive emotions and feelings of excitement, motivation, and inspiration. These emotions further reinforce the neural connections associated with your goals, making them more deeply ingrained in your subconscious mind.

Overall, a vision board serves as a powerful tool for reprogramming the subconscious mind by providing a tangible, visual representation of your aspirations and facilitating consistent focus and alignment with your goals.

7. Mindfulness and Meditation:

Practicing mindfulness and meditation can help in **observing and consciously changing patterns, attitudes, and beliefs present in the subconscious mind.**

By incorporating mindfulness into our daily routine, we can cultivate a greater awareness of **our thoughts and emotions,** leading to a deeper understanding of ourselves and the world around us.

Meditation, on the contrary, provides a space for **introspection and inner peace,** allowing us to tap into **our inner wisdom and foster a sense of calm and clarity in our lives.** Meditation is a practice that has been utilized for centuries to promote **relaxation, mindfulness, and inner peace.** It involves focusing our mind and eliminating the constant stream of thoughts that can often be overwhelming.

By setting aside time each day to meditate, individuals can **reduce stress, improve concentration, and enhance their overall well-being.** There are many different types of meditation techniques, such as **mindfulness meditation, guided visualization, and loving-kindness meditation,** each offering unique benefits for the **mind, body, and spirit.**

Through regular meditation practice, individuals can cultivate a sense of **calm and clarity, develop a deeper connection with themselves and others,** and ultimately lead a more balanced and fulfilling life. Whether practiced in a quiet room, a serene natural setting, or even during a busy day, meditation can be a powerful tool for self-discovery and personal growth.

Together, mindfulness and meditation offer powerful tools for personal growth and self-discovery, helping us to live more fully in the present moment and cultivate a greater sense of well-being.

How does meditation reprogram the subconscious mind?

Meditation can reprogram the subconscious mind through various mechanisms. When you meditate, you enter a state of deep relaxation and heightened awareness, which allows you to access and influence the subconscious mind more effectively.

1. **Increased mindfulness:** Meditation cultivates mindfulness, which involves paying attention to the present moment without judgment. By observing your thoughts, feelings, and sensations during meditation, you become more aware of the subconscious patterns and beliefs that influence your behavior and perception of reality.

2. **Positive affirmations and visualization:** During meditation, you can incorporate positive affirmations and visualization techniques to reprogram your subconscious mind. By repeatedly affirming positive beliefs and visualizing desired outcomes, you create **new neural pathways and overwrite old limiting beliefs stored in the subconscious.**

3. **Stress reduction:** Meditation reduces stress and activates the body's relaxation response, which helps to alleviate tension and anxiety stored in the subconscious mind. As stress diminishes, the subconscious becomes more receptive to positive suggestions and programming.

4. **Brainwave entrainment:** Different meditation techniques, such as mindfulness, focused attention, or loving-kindness meditation, can induce specific brainwave states associated with deep relaxation, heightened creativity, and increased receptivity to suggestions. These altered states of consciousness make the subconscious mind more open to positive reprogramming.

5. **Integration of insights and wisdom:** Through regular meditation practice, you develop greater self-awareness and insight into your thoughts, emotions, and behaviors. **This self-reflection allows you to identify and release subconscious patterns that no longer serve you while**

integrating new insights and wisdom into your subconscious programming.

Overall, meditation serves as a powerful tool for reprogramming the subconscious mind by promoting mindfulness, relaxation, positive affirmations, stress reduction, brainwave entrainment, and integration of insights. Through consistent practice, meditation can facilitate profound shifts in consciousness and behavior, leading to greater well-being and personal transformation.

In topic conclusion,

Techniques for Reprogramming the subconscious mind **to Practice the art of believing** are powerful tools for personal growth and transformation in various aspects of life. By consciously reshaping our deep-seated beliefs and attitudes through the techniques mentioned above like visualization, positive affirmations, repetition, etc. we can unlock our full potential and overcome self-limiting beliefs.

With dedication and persistence, we can cultivate a mindset that empowers us to achieve our goals and aspirations and live a more fulfilling life. Trusting in the process and committing to consistent practice are key to experiencing the transformative power of reprogramming the subconscious mind.

Remember, each person is unique, with varying emotional needs. Therefore, these techniques will be effective and vary from person to person, based on their mental capability, maturity, and adaptability to change and embrace the art of believing.

Other Psychological Techniques that Can Aid in Reprogramming the Subconscious Mind to Practice The Art of Believing.

1. Neuro-Linguistic Programming (NLP):

Neuro-Linguistic Programming (NLP) is a form of therapy and psychological technique that focuses on the connection between neurological processes, language, and behavioral patterns learned through experience.

It aims to help individuals reprogram their thoughts and behaviors to achieve personal growth and overcome obstacles. NLP techniques can be used to improve **communication skills, change negative beliefs, and enhance self-awareness.**

Understanding Neuro-Linguistic Programming (NLP):

Neuro: A neuron is a specialized cell in the nervous system that transmits information through electrical and chemical signals. Neurons are the basic building blocks of the brain, spinal cord, and nerves, and they play a crucial role in **processing and transmitting information throughout the body.**

Linguistic: Linguistic refers to the significance or interpretation assigned to words, phrases, or sentences within a particular language. It encompasses both denotative (literal) and connotative (implied or associated) meanings, as well as the context in which language is used. Linguistic meaning is a central concept in the study of semantics, which examines how words and sentences convey meaning within a language system.

Programming: often refers to the purpose or function of a particular piece of code, variable, function, or instructions. It can also refer to a cognitive process for telling a subconscious mind which tasks to perform to solve problems or deal with it. The meaning of programming constructs is closely tied to their intended behavior and their contribution to the overall functionality and logic of the human mind.

Neuro-linguistic programming (NLP) is a psychological approach that focuses on the connection between neurological processes ("neuro"), language ("linguistic"), and behavioral patterns learned through experience ("programming"). It suggests that by understanding and changing the ways we think (neuro), communicate (linguistic), and behave (programming), individuals can achieve personal and professional growth, improve communication skills, and overcome limiting beliefs or behaviors.

NLP techniques are often used in therapy, coaching, sales, education, and personal development. NLP techniques are various strategies and methods used to reprogram the individual's mind and behavior. NLP techniques are designed to tap into **the power of language and mindset to create positive changes in one's thoughts and actions.**

By utilizing a combination of **communication, sensory perception, and mental imagery,** NLP aims to help individuals **overcome limiting beliefs, phobias, and negative emotional patterns.** Through the practice of NLP, individuals can learn to **reframe their experiences, enhance their communication skills, and cultivate a more empowering mindset.**

Ultimately, NLP offers a pathway for personal growth, self-improvement, and transformation.

Some of the key NLP techniques include:

1. 1. Anchoring: Creating or associating a specific feeling, emotion, or state with a particular trigger or stimulus. Anchoring is a powerful psychological technique that can be utilized in various aspects of life.

By linking a specific feeling, emotion, or state with a particular trigger or stimulus, you can effectively influence your behavior or the behavior of others. This technique is often used in therapy, marketing, and even personal development to create positive associations and responses.

To use anchoring effectively, it is important to first identify the desired outcome or response you want to achieve. Then, choose a trigger or stimulus that can be consistently associated with that outcome. This trigger could be anything from a **specific word or gesture to a certain object or even a particular scent.**

Once you have established the anchor, it is crucial to consistently pair it with the **desired feeling or emotion.** Over time, **the association between the anchor and the response will become stronger,** ultimately leading to the desired outcome. By understanding and implementing the concept of anchoring, you can harness its power to shape behaviors, attitudes, and emotions in a positive and impactful way.

1.2. Reframing: Changing the meaning of a situation by looking at it from a different perspective. Reframing is a powerful tool that allows us to shift our mindset and see things in a new light. By changing our perspective, we can alter the meaning of a situation, opening up new possibilities and solutions. This technique can help us break free from limiting beliefs and find fresh ways to approach challenges. Embracing reframing can lead to greater creativity, resilience, and growth in both our personal and professional lives. So, next time you find yourself facing a difficult situation, remember the power of reframing and explore how a different viewpoint could transform your experience.

1.3. Swish Pattern: Replacing an undesirable behavior with a desired one by creating a mental image of the desired behavior and rapidly switching between the two. The Swish Pattern is a powerful technique used in Neuro-Linguistic Programming (NLP) to help replace unwanted behaviors with more desirable ones. By creating a vivid mental image of the desired behavior and repeatedly switching between this image and the unwanted behavior, individuals can effectively reprogram their minds to act in a more positive way.

To use the Swish Pattern, start by visualizing yourself engaging in the undesired behavior. Then, create a clear and detailed image of yourself successfully performing the desired behavior. As you focus on the positive image, quickly and vividly "swish" the unwanted behavior image to a small, distant spot in your mind. Repeat this process several times, increasing the speed of the swish each time.

With practice and consistency, the Swish Pattern can help you break free from negative habits and responses, allowing you to cultivate more constructive behaviors and achieve your desired goals. Remember to be patient with yourself and stay committed to the process as you work towards positive change.

1.4. Submodalities: Exploring and manipulating the sensory qualities of an experience, such as visual, auditory, and kinesthetic representations, for personal change. Submodalities are a powerful tool for personal growth and transformation. By delving into the sensory aspects of our experiences, such as how we see, hear, and feel things, we can gain a deeper understanding of ourselves and make positive changes in our lives.

Whether we are visualizing a goal, listening to our inner dialogue, or tapping into our emotions, exploring submodalities allows us to tweak and adjust these sensory qualities to create a more empowering and fulfilling experience. Through this process, we can enhance our perception, shift our mindset, and ultimately, shape our reality in a way that aligns with our desires and aspirations.

It's a fascinating journey of self-discovery and self-improvement, where we have the opportunity to fine-tune the building blocks of our thoughts, emotions, and behaviors to craft a life that truly resonates with who we are and what we want to become.

1.5. Parts Integration: Resolving internal conflicts by harmonizing conflicting parts of oneself. Parts integration is a powerful tool for personal growth and self-discovery. It involves recognizing and acknowledging the different aspects of oneself that may be in conflict and working towards finding a balance and harmony among these parts. By embracing and integrating these conflicting parts, individuals can achieve a sense of wholeness and inner peace. Through introspection, self-reflection, and perhaps even seeking support from a therapist or counselor, one can navigate their internal conflicts and work towards a more unified and authentic self. Embracing the complexities within oneself is a courageous step towards personal growth and emotional well-being.

1.6. Meta Model: A set of language patterns used to challenge and clarify old limiting beliefs and assumptions. The Meta Model is a powerful tool used in the field of neuro-linguistic programming (NLP) to help individuals identify and overcome limiting beliefs and assumptions that may be holding them back. By employing specific language patterns, the Meta Model aims to challenge and clarify these outdated thought patterns, allowing individuals to gain a deeper understanding of their beliefs and ultimately make positive changes in their lives.

Through the use of carefully crafted questions and techniques, the Meta Model encourages individuals to examine the language they use to describe their experiences and beliefs. By doing so, it enables them to uncover hidden presuppositions, generalizations, and distortions that may be contributing to their limitations. This heightened awareness can lead to a shift in perspective and pave the way for personal growth and transformation.

Incorporating the Meta Model into personal development practices can be a valuable way to enhance self-awareness, improve communication skills, and break free from self-imposed constraints. By embracing the principles of the Meta Model, individuals can embark on a journey of self-discovery and empowerment, allowing them to create a more fulfilling and authentic life.

1.7. Milton Model: A set of language patterns used to induce trance, create rapport, and facilitate communication. The Milton Model is a powerful tool utilized in the field of neurolinguistic programming to enhance communication and foster connections with others. By employing specific language patterns, individuals can effectively influence and persuade others, establish a sense of trust and rapport, and guide conversations in a way that promotes understanding and openness. Whether used in professional settings such as coaching or therapy, or in everyday interactions, mastering the Milton Model can greatly improve one's ability to communicate effectively and build stronger relationships.

1. 8. Hypnotic Language Patterns: Utilizing language patterns and suggestions to influence and persuade others. Hypnotic language patterns are a powerful tool in the art of communication. By carefully choosing your words and structuring your sentences, you can subtly influence and persuade others. These patterns work by tapping into the subconscious mind, planting seeds of suggestion that can lead to the desired outcome. When used ethically and responsibly, hypnotic language patterns can help create a positive impact in various aspects of life, from personal relationships to professional success. Remember, with great power comes great responsibility, so always use these techniques with integrity and respect for others.

1.9. Timeline Therapy: Using the concept of an individual's timeline to explore and change past experiences, resolve emotional issues, and set goals for the future. In Timeline Therapy, individuals are guided to visualize their past, present, and future along a mental timeline. By exploring significant events and emotions along this timeline, one can gain insights into how past experiences may be influencing current behaviors and beliefs. With the help of a skilled therapist or coach, individuals can work through unresolved emotions, release negative patterns, and create empowering beliefs to shape a more positive future. By utilizing this powerful technique, individuals can effectively make peace with their past, live fully in the present, and set meaningful goals for a brighter tomorrow.

1. 10. Rapport Building: Establishing and maintaining a deep level of connection and understanding with others by mirroring their physiology, tonality, and language patterns. Establishing and maintaining a deep level of connection and understanding with others is a fundamental skill in effective communication. It involves more than just words; it requires a genuine effort to connect on a deeper level. One powerful technique is mirroring, where you subtly reflect the other person's physiology, tonality, and language patterns. By doing so, you can create a sense of familiarity and trust, making it easier to build a strong rapport with them. Remember, genuine connection is not just about what you say, but how you make others feel. So, practice active listening, show empathy, and be authentic in your interactions to foster meaningful relationships.

2. Cognitive Restructuring

Cognitive restructuring is a therapeutic technique used in cognitive-behavioral therapy (CBT) to help individuals identify and change negative or maladaptive thought patterns. It involves challenging and reframing irrational or unhelpful thoughts that contribute to emotional distress and replacing them with more balanced and realistic thoughts. By changing these thought patterns, individuals can improve their emotional well-being and behavior.

How does cognitive restructuring reprogram the subconscious mind?

Cognitive restructuring involves identifying and challenging negative thought patterns and replacing them with more realistic and positive ones. Over time, this process can reprogram the subconscious mind by weakening the influence of negative beliefs and reinforcing positive ones, leading to more adaptive behaviors and emotional responses. This occurs through repeated practice and reinforcement of new thought patterns, and gradually reshaping the subconscious mind's automatic responses and beliefs.

Cognitive restructuring essentially rewires the subconscious mind by actively challenging and replacing negative or distorted beliefs with more balanced and rational ones. This process involves becoming aware of automatic negative thoughts, examining evidence for and against them, and generating more realistic and adaptive interpretations.

Through consistent practice and repetition, these new thought patterns become ingrained in the subconscious, gradually altering one's perception of themselves, others, and the world around them. This reprogramming occurs as the brain forms new neural connections and strengthens existing ones based on the revised cognitive schemas.

3. Repetition and Conditioning.

Consistently exposing oneself to **positive influences, affirmations, and actions** through repetition can gradually condition the subconscious mind to adopt new beliefs and behaviors.

How Does Repetition and Conditioning Reprogram the Subconscious Mind?

Repetition is the act of repeating or doing something over and over again. Psychology repetition can have various effects, it can help to **reinforce learning and memory as frequent repetition strengthens the connection between neurons in the brain.** Repetition can also Influence **perception and belief** as repeated exposure to certain stimuli can shape our attitudes and preferences.

Conditioning, on the other side, refers to the process of **learning an association between stimuli and responses.** It can be divided into classical conditioning and opponent conditioning.

1. **In classical conditioning,** an initially neutral stimulus is paired with an unconditional stimulus that naturally elicits a response. Over time, The neutral stimulus becomes a conditioned stimulus that can trigger a similar response.

2. **Operant conditioning involves learning based on consequences.** When a behavior is followed by a positive consequence (reinforcement), the behavior is more likely to be repeated. Conversely, when a behavior is followed by a negative consequence (punishment), the behavior is less likely to be repeated.

Operant conditioning is often used in **behavior modification** interventions and can be seen in everyday life, such as rewarding a child for good behavior or receiving a paycheck for completing work tasks. Conversely, when a behavior is followed by a negative consequence (punishment), the behavior is less likely to be repeated.

4. Hypnagogic State.

The hypnagogic state refers to the transitional state between wakefulness and sleep, typically occurring when a person is falling asleep. It is characterized by a variety of **sensory experiences, including hallucinations, vivid imagery, and feelings of floating or drifting.**

During this **unique state of consciousness,** individuals may perceive a blend of dream-like visuals and sounds that can be surreal and captivating. Some might experience fleeting moments of insight or creative inspiration, while others may encounter strange sensations that defy logic.

The hypnagogic state is a fascinating realm where the boundaries between reality and imagination blur, offering a glimpse into the mysterious workings of the mind. Embracing this liminal space can lead to unexpected discoveries and a deeper understanding of the subconscious mind's creative potential.

So, next time you find yourself on the brink of slumber, pay attention to the wonders that unfold in the hypnagogic state – you never know what hidden treasures your mind may uncover.

These experiences can be visual, auditory, tactile, or even conceptual. The hypnagogic state can be a vivid and immersive experience, similar to dreaming, but it is distinct from actual dreaming as it occurs while the person is still partially aware of their surroundings and their body's physical sensations.

How does the Hypnagogic State reprogram the subconscious mind?

The hypnagogic state, which occurs as one transitions from wakefulness to sleep, can be utilized for subconscious reprogramming through techniques such as **self-hypnosis or guided visualization.**

During this state, the subconscious mind becomes more receptive to suggestions and imagery, making it an ideal time to introduce positive affirmations or visualization exercises aimed at reprogramming deeply ingrained beliefs or habits.

By consistently accessing the hypnagogic state and delivering targeted suggestions aligned with desired changes, individuals can gradually reshape their subconscious patterns and behaviors over time. This process leverages the brain's heightened susceptibility to suggestion during this transitional phase of consciousness.

5. Emotional Freedom Techniques:

The Emotional Freedom Technique (EFT), also known as **"tapping,"** is a therapeutic technique that combines **elements of traditional Chinese acupuncture and modern psychology.** It is used to **alleviate emotional distress, reduce anxiety, and relieve physical pain.**

The Emotional Freedom Technique also known as tapping is a form of psychological acupressure that involves typing on specific Meridian points on the body while focusing on a particular negative emotion or a problem, aiming to release them and reprogram the subconscious mind.

It is based on the principle of **traditional Chinese medicine,** combined with a **modern psychological technique**. The purpose of EFT is to release and elevate negative emotional Trauma or old limiting beliefs by bringing harmony to **the body's energy system.** The taping process helps to re-balance the energy flow, Which is believed to **relieve emotional and physical Distress.**

EFT is often used to address various issues such as **anxiety, Stress, phobia, emotional trauma, pain relief, and more**. Tapping on the Meridian points is thought to stimulate the **body's energy system,** allowing for a shift in emotional state and promoting a sense of emotional freedom and relief.

The theory behind EFT is that tapping on these acupressure points helps release energy blockages and balance the body's energy systems. This, in turn, is believed to reduce negative emotions and promote emotional well-being.

EFT is often used for a variety of issues, including anxiety, stress, phobias, trauma, and chronic pain. While some individuals find it helpful, it's essential to recognize that the scientific evidence supporting ETf's effectiveness is mixed, and it may not be suitable for everyone.

It's advisable to consult a qualified mental health professional if you are experiencing severe emotional distress or mental health concerns. They can help you explore appropriate therapeutic approaches.

How do Emotional Freedom Techniques reprogram the subconscious mind?

Emotional Freedom Techniques (EFT) is a therapeutic approach that involves tapping on specific meridian points on the body while focusing on negative emotions or beliefs. This technique is thought to reprogram the subconscious mind by disrupting the body's energy system and releasing emotional blocks associated with negative experiences or beliefs.

As individuals tap on these meridian points, they bring attention to specific negative emotions or thoughts, effectively acknowledging and accepting them. This process can help to desensitize the emotional charge associated with these thoughts or memories. Additionally, while tapping, individuals often recite affirmations or positive statements that counteract the negative beliefs or emotions being addressed.

Over time, the repetitive tapping and affirmations can create new neural pathways in the brain, leading to a shift in underlying beliefs and emotional responses. By continuously practicing EFT, individuals can gradually reprogram their subconscious mind to adopt more positive and empowering beliefs, leading to improved emotional well-being and behavior.

In topic conclusion,

It is important to note: "Psychological Approaches" that reprogramming the subconscious mind may take time and consistency. It is recommended to work with a trained professional or engage in self-help resources that guide these techniques for safe and effective results.

VI. Healing and Subconscious Mind

A. Impact of the Subconscious Mind on Physical Health

The subconscious mind plays a significant role in determining our physical health as it can influence **our thoughts, emotions, behaviors, and overall well-being.**

Here are some ways in which the subconscious mind can impact physical health:

1. Stress and Anxiety: Negative thoughts and emotions stored in the subconscious mind can lead to chronic stress and anxiety, which can have a detrimental effect on the body. Prolonged stress can weaken the immune system, increase the risk of cardiovascular disease, and contribute to several other health issues.

2. Habits and Behaviors: The subconscious mind controls many of our habits and behaviors, some of which can impact our physical health. For instance, if we have negative beliefs about exercise or healthy eating stored in our subconscious, we may struggle to maintain a balanced diet or stay active, leading to health problems such as obesity or diabetes.

3. Physical Symptoms: The subconscious mind can also manifest physical symptoms in the body as a way of communicating unresolved emotional issues. For instance, chronic pain or digestive problems may be linked to repressed emotions stored in the subconscious mind.

4. Healing and Recovery: On the flip side, the subconscious mind can also play a positive role in promoting physical health and healing. By feeding the mind positive affirmations, visualizations, and beliefs, we can support the body's natural healing process and boost overall well-being.

The concept of self-healing was previously addressed in an earlier chapter. Please refer back to it to refresh your memory.

When we harness the power of the subconscious mind to focus on positivity, we can encourage a sense of well-being and aid in the healing process. Positive affirmations, visualizations, and beliefs have the potential to uplift our spirits and promote physical health.

By nurturing a mindset of healing and restoration, we pave the way for a journey towards improved wellness and vitality. Trust in the innate capacity of your body to heal, and let your subconscious mind be a guiding force in your path to recovery.

Overall, it is important to be mindful of the impact of the subconscious mind on physical health and work towards releasing negative emotions, beliefs, and patterns stored in the subconscious to achieve optimal health and wellness.

B. Role of the subconscious mind in healing past trauma and negative experiences.

The subconscious mind plays a critical role in healing past trauma and negative experiences. Trauma and negative experiences can **cause deep emotional wounds** that often linger in the subconscious mind, creating ongoing distress and affecting **one's mental and emotional well-being.**

One way the subconscious mind aids in healing trauma is through memory processing and integration. Traumatic memories are often stored in the subconscious mind in fragmented and disorganized ways, leading to flashbacks, nightmares, and other symptoms of post-traumatic stress disorder (PTSD).

Through various therapeutic techniques such as EMDR (Eye Movement Desensitization and Reprocessing) or somatic experiencing, the subconscious mind can be gently guided to process and integrate these memories more cohesively and adaptively, reducing the emotional charge and distress associated with them.

Moreover, the subconscious mind is also responsible for housing core beliefs and thought patterns that may have been formed as a result of past traumatic experiences. These beliefs and patterns can perpetuate negative self-perceptions, self-sabotaging behaviors, and feelings of unworthiness or helplessness.

By engaging in therapies such as cognitive-behavioral therapy or mindfulness-based practices, individuals can work to reprogram these maladaptive beliefs and thought patterns at a subconscious level, leading to lasting healing and transformation.

Additionally, the subconscious mind is highly receptive to positive affirmations, visualization, and guided imagery, making it a powerful tool for reprogramming the mind and cultivating resilience and self-compassion. By consistently engaging in these practices, individuals can cultivate a more positive and empowering mindset, fostering greater healing and growth in the face of past trauma and negative experiences.

In summary, the subconscious mind plays a crucial role in healing past trauma and negative experiences by processing and integrating traumatic memories, reprogramming maladaptive beliefs and thought patterns, and fostering resilience and self-compassion through positive affirmations and visualization.

By tapping into the power of the subconscious mind, individuals can embark on a transformative healing journey and cultivate a greater sense of empowerment and overall well-being.

In Topic Conclusion:

The subconscious mind plays a significant role in shaping our thoughts, behaviors, and emotions, often influencing our actions without our conscious awareness. Its complexity and influence highlight the importance of understanding and harnessing its power for personal growth and development.

The subconscious mind is a powerful force that can greatly influence our healing and recovery journey. By understanding its role and learning to work with it, we can tap into its potential and promote physical and emotional well-being.

It is essential to pay attention to our thoughts and beliefs, address any past traumas, and practice positive thinking and visualization techniques. With the right mindset and tools, we can harness the power of our subconscious mind to support us on the path toward healing and recovery.

Part II:
Spiritual Aspects

I. Spiritual Aspects of "The Art of Believing".

Let's discover a few takeover points, that might help you lead a peaceful life:

- **A. The Art of Believing: Let's Embark on a Journey to Establishing Relationships with Higher Self.**
  - **How to connect with a higher self?**
  - **How can you recognize when your higher self tries to communicate with you?**
  - **Understanding the Higher Self**
- **B. Common challenges to building a relationship with a higher self.**
- **C. Strategies to rebuild the relationship with the Higher self.**

II. Prayer for Practicing "The Art of Believing".

III. My Personal Experience On "Embarking The Art of Believing.

IV. Evaluation of the Art of Believing.

A. The Art of Believing: Let's Embark on a Journey to Establishing Relationships with Higher Self

In our fast-paced and chaotic world, it is easy to lose sight of our true selves. We are often preoccupied with worldly demands, societal expectations, and external validations. However, beneath these layers, lies our higher self – a source of wisdom, clarity, and inner peace.

Building a relationship with our higher self is an art, one that allows us to tap into our **true potential, discover our life purpose, and experience profound personal growth**. This journey requires belief – **belief in ourselves, belief in a higher power, and belief in the transformative power of self-connection.**

In this guide, we will explore the art of believing and provide you with tools and insights to embark on this transformative journey of building a relationship with your higher self.

Exploring the Concept of Higher Self: The concept of the higher self is often associated with spirituality and personal growth. It refers to a deeper aspect of ourselves that transcends our physical existence and connects us to a higher power or universal consciousness.

The higher self is often described as a wiser and more virtuous version of ourselves, representing our truest and highest potential. It is believed to hold a greater understanding of the world, our life purpose, and the path toward self-fulfillment.

Connecting with the higher self involves an inner journey of self-discovery and introspection. It requires quieting the **mind, practicing mindfulness, and tuning into our intuition.** By aligning with our higher self, we can tap into its wisdom, guidance, and clarity to navigate our lives with greater purpose and authenticity.

People may seek to cultivate a relationship with their higher self to gain a deeper understanding of themselves, find answers to life's questions, make important decisions, and access a sense of inner peace and spiritual fulfillment.

It is important to note that the concept of the higher self can vary across different belief systems and spiritual practices. Some may interpret it as a divine aspect within themselves, while others may see it as a connection to a higher power or universal consciousness.

1. How to connect with a higher self?

Connecting with your higher self is a deeply personal and spiritual journey. Here are some steps you can follow to begin connecting with your higher self:

1.1. Create a Quiet and Sacred Space: Find a quiet and peaceful place where you can be alone without distractions. This could be a corner in your home, a meditation room, or a natural outdoor setting.

1.2. Meditation and Mindfulness: Practice regular meditation or mindfulness techniques to quiet your mind, increase awareness, and cultivate a connection with your higher self. Start with deep breathing exercises, focusing on your breath, and gradually progress to longer periods of meditation.

1.3. Journaling and Self-Reflection: Keep a journal to record your thoughts, dreams, and experiences. Reflect on these entries to gain insights into your higher self and its guidance. Ask yourself thought-provoking questions and write down your answers intuitively.

1.4. Intuition and Inner Guidance: Learn to trust your intuition and inner guidance. Pay attention to the subtle signals, feelings, or "gut instincts" that arise within you. This is your higher self communicating with you.

1.5. Visualization and Affirmations: Practice visualizing yourself connected to your higher self. Visualize a radiant light surrounding you, filling you with wisdom, love, and guidance. Repeat affirmations such as "I am connected to my higher self" to strengthen this connection.

1.6. Seek Spiritual Practices: Explore different spiritual practices such as yoga, energy healing, chanting, or prayer to enhance your spiritual connection and reach a higher state of consciousness that allows for communication with your higher self.

1.7. Seek Guidance from Spiritual Mentors or Guides: If you feel stuck or unsure in your journey, seek guidance from spiritual mentors, life coaches, or guidance counselors who can help you navigate your spiritual path.

Remember, connecting with your higher self is a lifelong journey and may take time, patience, and dedication. Be open to the process and trust that the connection will deepen as you continue to explore and learn.

2. How can you recognize when your higher self tries to communicate with you?

Connecting with your higher self is a deeply personal and subjective experience, and everyone may have their unique ways of knowing when their higher self is communicating with them. However, **here are some common signs or experiences that may indicate a connection with your higher self:**

2.1 Intuition and Inner Guidance: Your higher self often communicates through feelings of intuition or gut instincts. You might have a strong sense of knowing or deep inner guidance directing you toward certain choices or actions.

2.2 Synchronicities and Signs: You may start noticing meaningful coincidences or synchronicities in your life, such as repeatedly seeing certain numbers or symbols, hearing specific songs or phrases, or encountering people who provide guidance or answers to your questions.

2.3 Inner Voice or Thoughts: Your higher self might communicate through a clear, calm, and wise inner voice that feels different from your regular mental chatter. It can provide insights, guidance, and hindsight on situations, often lovingly and compassionately.

2.4 Dreams and Visions: Your higher self might communicate through vivid dreams or visions that feel meaningful, vivid, or emotionally charged. Pay attention to recurring themes, symbols, or messages that may arise during your dream state.

2.5 Strong Emotional Resonance: When your higher self communicates, you may experience a deep sense of resonance, alignment, or harmony within yourself. It might feel like a profound sense of truth, peace, or joy that comes with the message or guidance received.

2.6 Body Sensations and Energy Shifts: Pay attention to any physical sensations or energetic shifts that occur when you are seeking guidance or connecting with your higher self. It can manifest as a warm or tingling sensation, chills, or a feeling of expansion.

Remember, connecting with your higher self requires practice, trust, and openness. It's important to cultivate a sense of discernment and trust your own inner knowing when determining if your higher self is communicating with you.

3. Understanding the Higher Self

Here we delve into the concept of the higher self. By understanding what the higher self represents, we can begin to grasp its significance in our journey toward self-discovery and personal growth.

3.1. Cultivating Belief in Ourselves

Belief in ourselves is the foundation of building a relationship with our higher self. In this book, we already explored practical techniques to cultivate self-belief. From embracing self-compassion to challenging self-limiting beliefs, we unveiled the power within us to create a strong sense of self-belief that aligns us with our higher self.

Trusting in a Higher Power

Trusting in a higher power, whether it be a divine entity or the universe itself, can provide solace and guidance along our journey. In this book, we explored the ways to cultivate trust in a higher power, strengthen our faith, and surrender to the wisdom and guidance that it offers.

Connecting with the Higher Self

Building a relationship with our higher self requires dedicated effort and practice. In this book, we delved into various techniques, rituals, and meditative practices that foster a deeper connection with our higher self. From journaling to mindfulness, we unveil the tools that enable us to tap into our inner wisdom and gain clarity in our path.

Nurturing the Relationship

Once we have established a connection with our higher self, it is essential to nurture and deepen this relationship continuously. In this chapter, we discuss the importance of self-care, regular self-reflection, and mindfulness practices to foster a harmonious bond with our higher self.

In Topic Conclusion:

Building a relationship with our higher self is a lifelong journey. It is an art that requires commitment, belief, and practice. As we cultivate self-belief, trust in a higher power, and connect deeply with our inner wisdom, we unlock the transformative power that lies within us. In this guide, we have explored the art of believing and provided practical tools and insights to embark on this profound journey.

Remember, the path to building a relationship with your higher self is unique to you, but with dedication and belief, it will lead you to a life of fulfillment, purpose, and self-discovery.

We are all born with the capacity to believe in something bigger than ourselves. Whether it's a higher power, a higher purpose, or our potential, the act of believing can lead us to a successful life. This is the art of believing.

B. Common challenges to building a relationship with a higher self.

Building a relationship with a higher self can be a challenging process, but it is an essential step in the journey of self-discovery and growth. While it may seem like an impossible task, several common challenges can be overcome with patience and determination.

The first challenge is having a clear understanding of what the higher self is. Many people believe that the higher self is some kind of spiritual or supernatural being, but this is not the case. The higher self is simply the part of you that knows and understands your true purpose in life, and it exists within each of us. It is important to understand that your higher self does not exist outside of you, but rather, it is within you.

The second challenge in building a relationship with your higher self is learning to listen. Many people struggle with listening to their inner voice because they are so busy with their day-to-day lives. It can be hard to take the time to be still and listen to what your higher self is telling you. It takes practice and patience to learn how to quiet your mind and open yourself up to receive guidance from your higher self.

The third challenge is trusting that what your higher self is telling you is true. We can often be skeptical of our inner voice, especially if we have faced difficult times in our lives. We may feel that we know better than our higher selves, but it's important to listen and trust that our inner guidance can help us make wise decisions. Trusting in the wisdom of our higher selves can be difficult, but with practice, we can learn to trust it more fully.

The fourth challenge in building a relationship with your higher self is finding the courage to act on its guidance. Listening to your higher self can be an intimidating process, as it often leads us down a path that requires us to confront difficult emotions or make challenging decisions. It can be tempting to ignore or push away this inner guidance, but it's important to find the courage to take action on what you hear from your higher self. Even if it's uncomfortable or difficult in the short term, following guidance from your higher self will ultimately lead you down the path of true happiness and fulfillment.

Finally, the fifth challenge in building a relationship with your higher self is allowing yourself to accept its guidance without judgment or second-guessing. It's natural to doubt or second-guess yourself when you are exploring new territory, but this should not prevent you from acting on the guidance of your higher self. Instead, accept what you hear without judgment and trust in its wisdom.

Building a relationship with your higher self takes time and patience, but it can be an incredibly rewarding process. By understanding what the higher self is, learning how to listen, trusting its guidance, finding the courage to act on it, and accepting its wisdom without judgment, you will be able to build a strong relationship with your higher self that will serve as a source of strength and guidance throughout your life journey.

C. Strategies to rebuild the relationship with the Higher self.

Rebuilding the relationship with your Higher Self involves practices that promote self-awareness, mindfulness, and inner alignment.

Here are some strategies to help:

1. **Meditation:** Dedicate regular time to quieting the mind and connecting with your inner self through meditation. This practice can help you listen to your intuition and access deeper wisdom.

2. **Journaling:** Reflect on your thoughts, emotions, and experiences through journaling. This allows you to explore your inner landscape, identify patterns, and gain insights into your true desires and aspirations.

3. **Mindfulness:** Cultivate mindfulness in your daily life by being fully present in each moment. Pay attention to your thoughts, feelings, and sensations without judgment, allowing you to deepen your connection with your Higher Self.

4. **Self-Reflection:** Set aside time for introspection to evaluate your values, beliefs, and goals. Consider how your actions align with your authentic self and make adjustments as necessary to honor your true essence.

5. **Soulful Activities:** Engage in activities that nourish your soul and bring you joy, whether it's spending time in nature, creating art, practicing yoga, or listening to uplifting music.

6. **Inner Dialogue:** Develop a loving and compassionate inner dialogue with yourself. Treat yourself with kindness

and understanding, nurturing a supportive relationship with your Higher Self.

7. Seek Guidance: Seek guidance from spiritual teachers, mentors, or trusted friends who can provide support and perspective on your journey of self-discovery and spiritual growth.

8. Connect with Spirituality: Explore spiritual practices and teachings that resonate with you, such as mindfulness meditation, yoga, prayer, or energy healing. Connect with a higher power or universal intelligence that aligns with your beliefs.

9. Set Intentions: Set clear intentions for your growth and transformation, expressing your desire to deepen your connection with your Higher Self and live in alignment with your true purpose.

10. Trust and Surrender: Trust in the wisdom of your Higher Self and surrender to the flow of life. Allow yourself to let go of control and surrender to the guidance and support of your inner wisdom.

By incorporating these strategies into your life, you can rebuild and strengthen your relationship with your Higher Self, leading to greater clarity, fulfillment, and alignment with your true essence.

In Topic Conclusion.

Spirituality is an expansive subject that cannot be fully explored in a single chapter. It requires time to comprehend and integrate into our lives.

Life presents various perspectives: logical minds shape our reality on one side, while spirituality offers deeper insights into the unseen world and provides significant support during challenging times on the other side.

In our upcoming second volume, **"The Art Of Believing -A Journey To A Peaceful Life,"** we will delve into further captivating facets of spirituality and how they influence our lives. Stay tuned to discover the hidden truths, reinforce belief in the Higher Self, combat uncertainty, and enhance sustainability in a world filled with tranquility.

The most captivating section of Volume 2 will leave you spellbound. Experience the awe-inspiring story of a 23-year-old boy Sunny, who conquered death with the intervention of supreme power, and discover how spirituality plays a vital role in such cases. Brace yourself for more enthralling true stories that showcase the indomitable power of the human spirit. Get ready for an unforgettable journey!

II. Prayer for Practicing "The Art of Believing".

Prayer for Emotional and Physical Healing.

Dear Heavenly Father,

I come before you today with a humble and open heart, seeking your guidance and strength. I acknowledge that you are the source of all healing and that your power and love are limitless.

Father, I confess that at times I struggle to believe in the possibility of my own healing. Doubts and fears fill my mind, causing me to question if I will ever find relief from this physical ailment that plagues me.

But today, Lord, I choose to surrender those doubts and fears to you. I choose to believe that you can bring forth restoration and wholeness in my life. I choose to place my trust in your promise that you have plans to prosper me and not to harm me, to give me hope and a future (Jeremiah 29:11).

Help me, Lord, to fix my gaze on you and not on my circumstances. It fills me with faith to believe that even when human reasoning tells me that my healing is impossible, you are the God of the impossible. As I lift my petitions to you, may your peace that surpasses all understanding guard my heart and mind in Christ Jesus (Philippians 4:7).

Father, I pray for your compassion and mercy to be poured out upon me. I ask that you grant me the strength and patience to endure this season of waiting, knowing that your timing is perfect. Increase my faith and help me to lean not on my own understanding, but to acknowledge you in all my ways so that you can direct my paths (Proverbs 3:5-6).

Lord, I am ready to receive your healing touch. I humbly ask that you grant me healing according to your will. In whatever way you choose to manifest your healing power in my life, may it bring glory and honor to your name.

Thank you, Lord, for your abounding love and countless blessings. I am grateful for the gift of salvation through Jesus Christ, and I trust that in his name, I can be healed. I pray all these things in faith, believing that you will accomplish more than I can ask or imagine.

In your name, I pray. Amen.

Prayer to overcome suffering.

Dear Heavenly Father,

I come before you with a heavy heart, burdened by suffering and pain. I ask for your strength and guidance to help me overcome these trials.

May your grace and love surround me in this difficult time, reassuring me of your presence and support. Help me to have faith that you will never abandon me, no matter how tough the road may be.

Grant me the courage to face my challenges head-on, trusting in your plan for me and finding peace in knowing that you are with me every step of the way.

I surrender my pain and suffering to you, Lord, knowing that you are the ultimate healer and source of comfort. Help me to find solace in your promises and to emerge from this trial stronger than ever before.

In your name, I pray. Amen.

Prayer for Success and Aspirations.

Dear Heavenly Father,

I come before you today with a humble heart, seeking your guidance, wisdom, and strength as I strive for success and pursue my aspirations.

I pray that you would bless my efforts and help me to stay focused and diligent in the pursuit of my goals. I ask for your divine favor to open doors of opportunity and to grant me success in all that I do.

May you grant me the courage to step out of my comfort zone and to take risks in pursuit of my dreams. Help me to trust in your plan for my life and to let go of any fears or doubts that may hold me back.

I pray for wisdom to make wise decisions, perseverance to overcome challenges, and patience to trust in your perfect timing.

May you grant me the strength to stay committed to my goals, even when the road ahead seems difficult. Help me to stay humble in success and gracious in failure.

I entrust my hopes and dreams into your hands, knowing that you are the ultimate source of all success and fulfillment.

In your name, I pray. Amen.

Prayer for financial stability

Dear Heavenly Father,

I come to you today with a heavy heart, burdened by the weight of financial stress and worries. I pray for your guidance and wisdom as I navigate the challenges of achieving financial stability.

Please help me to make wise decisions with my finances, spend wisely, and save diligently. Grant me the strength and perseverance to work diligently and responsibly to provide for myself and my loved ones.

I pray for your provision and blessing in my endeavors, that I may be able to meet my financial obligations and enjoy a life of abundance and security.

Please ease my anxieties and fears about money, and help me to trust in your plan for my life. Grant me peace and confidence in knowing that you are always with me, guiding and supporting me through all of life's challenges.

In your name, I pray. Amen.

Prayer to overcome the adversities in life.

Dear Heavenly Father,

I come to you humbly, seeking strength and guidance in overcoming the adversities I face. You know the challenges that I am currently dealing with, and I ask for your help in finding the courage and perseverance to overcome them.

Please grant me the wisdom to navigate through these difficult times and the patience to trust in your plan for me. Give me the strength to push through the obstacles in my path and the faith to believe that better days are ahead.

I know that with your love and support, I can conquer any adversity that comes my way. I trust in your goodness and mercy, and I surrender myself to your will.

Thank you for always being by my side, even in my darkest moments. I know that with you, all things are possible.

In your name, I pray. Amen.

III. My Personal Experience On "Embarking The Art Of Believing."

I started my belief journey at age 15, and it has increased and deepened as age grows. Belief is a powerful force that has guided me through the ups and downs of life. As I embarked on my journey to -The Art of Believing at the age of 15, I never could have imagined the profound impact it would have on me. With each passing year, my faith has only grown stronger and deeper, anchoring me in times of uncertainty and lifting me in moments of doubt.

One of the most transformative aspects of my belief journey has been the healing stories that have unfolded along the way. From moments of profound clarity to instances of miraculous intervention, each story serves as a testament to the power of faith and the resilience of the human spirit.

I have learned that believing is not just about having faith in something greater than ourselves; it's about trusting in the inherent goodness of the universe and the boundless potential that lies within each of us. Through "The Art of Believing," I have discovered a sense of peace, purpose, and connection that has truly enriched my life in ways I never thought possible.

As I continue on this journey, I carry these belief-healing stories with me as a source of inspiration and strength. They remind me that no matter what challenges may come my way, I have the power to overcome them with unwavering faith and a steadfast belief in the infinite possibilities that lie ahead.

In Earlier Context, I highlighted the significance of beliefs. I had a profound experience during **"The Art of Believing -**

Learning Journey", which I am excited to share with you. I hope that it will motivate you to navigate challenging situations and circumstances.

All mentioned stories have a unique power to inspire, comfort, and guide you through difficult times. They serve as reminders that:

"Even in our darkest moments, there is always hope for a brighter tomorrow."

As I reflect on my own journey, I recall a moment that deeply impacted me and shaped the way I approach life's challenges. I believe that by sharing those experiences with you, one can find strength in knowing that we are not alone in our struggles. Let's embrace the lessons learned and move forward with courage and resilience.

"Congratulations on your progress towards a better future! You are already on the right track, and there are even more opportunities ahead waiting for you to explore and achieve your desired life."

IV. Evaluation of the Art of Believing

"The Art of Believing- A Journey to A Peaceful Life", is a book written by Dr. Sunita Raaj, A Health Professional, Self-Healing Advocate, Empowerment Coach & Author.

Dr. Sunita Raaj is a Health professional, a self-healing advocate, an empowerment coach, and an author dedicated to helping individuals harness their inner strength and resilience. With holistic healing practices and personal transformation, She brings a unique blend of wisdom, compassion, and practical guidance to her work.

She believes in the innate healing potential within each person and she is passionate about empowering others to tap into their inner resources to create positive change in their lives.

In this book, she outlines the importance of positive thinking and how it can lead to success in the various aspects of life and overcome all circumstances. She draws from both scientific and spiritual sources to illustrate her points and help readers learn how to make positive thinking an integral part of their lives.

This book provides an in-depth look at how the power of belief can be used to achieve success in various areas of life. And how to connect with a higher- self or universe, to unlock the doors of opportunities, This book provides practical steps to cultivate positive beliefs and effectively apply them to achieve personal goals and aspirations.

It covers powerful techniques such as creating affirmations for positive change, staying highly motivated and productive, using visualization techniques to manifest

desired outcomes, and reprogramming the subconscious mind to facilitate the healing of any illness or disease.

The book is filled with examples from people who have used the power of belief to achieve their goals. There are also a variety of activities that readers can use to reinforce the concepts they learn in the book, such as writing down affirmations or creating a vision board.

The Art of Believing is an excellent resource for anyone looking to make positive changes in their lives. It provides valuable information about how the power of belief can be used to create success, as well as practical advice on how to put this knowledge into practice.

The book also includes inspiring stories from people who have achieved success through believing in themselves, which can help motivate those who may be struggling with self-doubt.

In conclusion, The Art of Believing is an incredibly useful and inspiring book. It contains valuable advice that readers can use to create lasting positive changes in their lives.

The examples and activities included throughout the book are also highly useful for reinforcing the concepts taught in the text. Furthermore, the inspiring stories from those who have achieved success through the power of belief are incredibly motivating and can help give readers the boost they need to go after their goals.

Overall, The Art of Believing is an excellent resource for anyone looking to make meaningful changes in their lives and become more successful through the power of belief. With its detailed advice and inspiring stories, it is sure to be a valuable addition to any bookshelf.